Justin Hill was born in Freeport, G███████ North Yorkshire. He spent seven year████████ China and Eritrea, before returning ████████ *Dream Teahouse* (winner of a Betty ████████ Memorial Prize), which has been tr███████ banned in China. *Ciao Asmara* was s█████ ██████ the Thomas Cook Travel Award 2003.

Praise for *Ciao Asmara*

'His valediction has all the bitter-sweet anger and gratitude of Orwell's escape from Barcelona, even down to his homecoming glimpse of "impossibly green" English fields and plump cows. It helps to close a tale that strikes a plangent note of regret without recrimination, and clarity without cynicism' *Independent*

'Justin Hill can write – and he has a story to tell, too. Hill is mesmerised by the landscape, the people and their stories, and goes into much detail on the country's recent political and military history' Anthony Sattin, *Sunday Times*

'This incredibly emotional book describes the experiences of novelist and former aid worker Justin Hill . . . Hill is a great and passionate storyteller, and his account is both readable and important' *Independent on Sunday*

'Expressive of a deep pain for lost hope, lost dreams, lost lives' Ian Finlayson, *The Times*

'This book is a love letter to the country he had to leave . . . [Hill] isn't striving for impartiality, but rather to give a glimpse of how it feels, tastes and smells to live there. The tone is low-key, but the story it tells is anything but that: a brief and beautiful moment of calm between storms' *Sunday Times*

'*Ciao Asmara* has much to recommend it. Hill is a strong writer . . . *Ciao Asmara* offers an excellent starting point for readers. It is a reliable and often moving book' *Sunday Business Post* (Ireland)

'Hill's account of his time working as a teacher in Eritrea is an accomplished piece of travel writing. Lured by the promise of making a difference, Hill brings a novelistic eye to a new country with a long past' *Sunday Herald* (Glasgow)

Also by Justin Hill

A Bend in the Yellow River
The Drink and Dream Teahouse

Ciao Asmara

A Classic Account of Contemporary Africa

Justin Hill

An *Abacus* Book

First published in Great Britain as a paperback original
by Abacus in 2002

This edition published by Abacus in 2004

Copyright © Justin Hill 2002

The moral right of the author has been asserted.

The extract from *The Diaries of Evelyn Waugh*, edited by Michael
Davie, is reprinted by kind permission of Weidenfeld & Nicolson

All pictures are the author's own except for the following:
Page 30: Emperor Haile Selassie: Popperfoto
Page 38: Lt-Col Mengistu Haile Mariam: Camera Press
Page 48: EPLF soldiers: Mike Wells/Camera Press
Page 129: Old bank and governor's palace, Massawa

A CIP catalogue record for this book
is available from the British Library.

ISBN 0 349 11774 8

Typeset in Sabon by M Rules

Map by John Gilkes

Printed and bound in Great Britain
by Clays Ltd, St Ives plc

Abacus
An imprint of
Time Warner Book Group UK
Brettenham House
Lancaster Place
London WC2E 7EN

www.twbg.co.uk

for the letter M
and the number
42

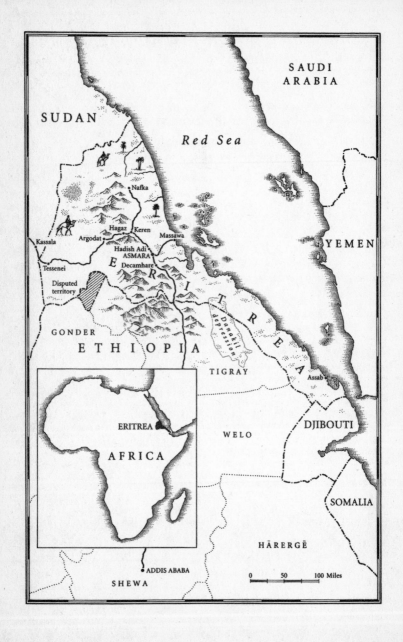

I

In the autumn of 1989 a profound tremor upset the world. The epicentre was definitely located in Russia, west of the Urals, but the shockwaves were much more keenly felt in mainland Europe. In all the countries of the world, people gathered around their TV sets and followed their daily news. The Berlin Wall crumbled; Stalinist hard-liners walked as free men out of Prague Castle; in Romania, President Ceauşescu and his wife were arrested and blindfolded and put on trial.

Ceauşescu took his wife by the arm and felt his way into the brick yard, presidential toe leading. He stood up against the wall; his servants lined up opposite him, loaded their rifles and shot him dead. The guns were loud in the bare brick yard. His red shadow dripped down the wall as his wife filled his place. For a second time the guns aimed and fired in chorus.

Both their bodies were hauled away and their shades were washed from the red brick wall. The cameras were turned off; the video released for the Christmas Day news.

In Africa there were massacres, civil wars and optimistic peace treaties. Behind the colonial façades they had inherited, presidents-for-life sweated in their sleep and woke to the sound of angry murmurs of popular discontent. Some of them lost their nerve and fled. Others, like Ceauşescu, were not given the chance. As each post-colonial ruler fell, people gathered in their shanty towns and cheered. 'Our second liberation!'

Their African Renaissance.

The most potent symbol of this blaze of change was the referendum held in north-east Ethiopia on 23–5 April 1993. The vote was to provide 'a legal and democratic conclusion' to the long struggle for independence of Eritrea, an ex-Italian colony governed by Ethiopia since 1950. The question, which was written in the Arabic and Ge'ez scripts, read: 'Do you want Eritrea to be an independent and sovereign country?'

For those who could not read, the government of freedom fighters had posters in every street in the country. The choice before them was colour-coded for the illiterate. 'No' was red. Ethiopian soldiers with armfuls of skulls patrolled the perimeter of the poster. Their faces were fierce, their guns dripped blood. They bit cigarettes in their grinning teeth and cast lustful eyes over the women. Continued life in Ethiopia would be endless war – burnt villages, dismembered bodies.

'Yes' was blue. It showed happy babies, fields of abundant wheat, and Soviet-style images of peace and prosperity. The EPLF (Eritrean People's Liberation Front), who had led the people out of a thirty-year war, were showing them the Promised Land. It was a Free Eritrea.

Illiterate women left purdah for the first time in their lives to attach their thumbprints to ballot papers they couldn't read. Crooked walking sticks took old men by the hand and led them to the place of voting. Even the fierce and solitary shepherds came down off their thorny mountainsides, with goats in tow. They had their long, carved combs in their black afros, tilted forward at aggressive angles. Their dirty jalabias were the robes of kings: they ignored the long queues and walked straight up to the clerk's desk. Nobody dared stop them.

On the day the results were due to be announced there was a tense air of expectation. Women sat on woven carpets, drinking syrupy-thick coffee and tossing popcorn into their mouths. The men put on their suits and went to slurp cappuccino in the old Italian cafés. All listened as the UN observers declared the referendum 'free and fair'. The turnout of eligible voters was 98.5 per cent. There was silence while the newsreader got around to announcing the result. Even the cappuccino machines were turned off.

After a long preamble, the moment everyone was waiting for arrived: the announcer reported that the people of Eritrea had voted a resounding 99.81 per cent in favour of independence from Ethiopia. It was the most affirmative referendum in the history of mankind.

The independence celebrations were universally covered by the world's media. Foreign correspondents relished the chance to feed the people at home a sweet story of hope and reconstruction. The charm of Eritrea was its quiet determination to build itself, not rely on aid hand-outs.

This independence came from the Eritreans' long history of being ignored by the rest of the world. The indifference and neglect they had suffered had left them with a ferocious sense of individuality. They were as uncompromising as their hard

and stony mountains. They had won the war unaided; they
would rebuild their country unaided too.

When the government appealed for international help, they
vetted the offers of aid. 'Aid' linked to industrial or defence
contracts was refused. 'Aid' linked to the right to prospect for
oil or gold was ignored. 'Aid' that was channelled back to the
donating country was spurned. 'Aid' organisations that spent
most of their money on expat salaries, not on the people they
were supposed to help, were denied permission to operate in
Eritrea.

Eritrea's unconventionality in all things was exemplified
by the Minister for Transport, who was to be found with his
jacket off, helping in the reconstruction, pausing to hold quick
interviews, then returning with his pickaxe to his place in the
ranks of labourers.

The inside pages of the international monthlies, Sunday
supplements and glossy magazines were full of eulogising
copy. A country that had defeated both the world's super-
powers in the cruel and relentless thirty-year war. A country
liberated by an army of volunteer freedom fighters, a third of
whom were women.

Eritrea suddenly found itself 'a news story'.

———

I was a volunteer aid worker. When my contract in China ran
out I looked at the world map and checked with friends for
available jobs. One sent me details of a teaching post in a
remote Malawian school. There were ten Malawian teachers,
and six other aid workers: two Jesuits, two Italian nuns and a
German couple. It looked too crowded. Most other jobs I

found in Africa were the same: long programmes with hordes of aid workers. It wasn't aid so much as dependency.

It was then that I began to hear tales of Eritrea. An exciting new country, defeating the stereotypes of Africa as corrupt, war-torn or hopeless. It was a country where volunteers were desperately needed, where people were united to help build their new society, where aid was used to enable the people to help themselves. A unique opportunity to see a country being born.

Then I met a girl who'd been teaching in Eritrea. From the way she spoke I saw she'd fallen in love with the place. Eritrea had given her life new purpose: the hard work of the people; the devotion they had to a cause higher than personal profit or career advancement; their unshakeable optimism.

I signed up.

One March morning I got out of bed, went downstairs and found the morning's post scattered under the letterbox. There was a letter offering me a teaching post in Eritrea starting in July 1996. There was a visa application form and a list of necessary injections. I read the letter as I put on the kettle.

The tea was still brewing when my mother came down. She sat and slowly rubbed her eyes while I poured. Both of us clutched our steaming mugs against the cold spring morning which dripped outside. Between us, on the table, the letter lay open.

'I'm going to Eritrea,' I said.

'Oh,' she said, then yawned. 'Do you have to go so soon?'

'It's not so far away.'

She yawned again, then looked up and said, 'Where *is* Eritrea?'

I showed her the map. Eritrea lay like a long, broad dagger, poised over northern Ethiopia and stretching half the length of the Red Sea, all the way down to where its southern mouth opened out into the Indian Ocean.

'Where will you be going to?' my mother asked.

'Keren,' I said.

The black dot named 'Keren' lay in the middle of the country.

My mother took a label and stuck it on to the map. On it she wrote my name. Keren was no longer Keren, it was Justin.

———————

My plane flew from Heathrow.

We crossed Europe and the Mediterranean, and continued flying due south. For an hour we followed the Nile, a fragile blue ribbon in the waves of sand. On one side of the plane was the red-orange glow of another day, and on the other the dark cool of midnight. We were approaching the northern edge of the Ethiopian highlands, the Tibet of Africa: a cultural spaghetti junction where Africa and Arabia, Muslim and Christian and Animist all mix and meet.

The Ethiopian highlands used to be the Garden of Eden: a land that was once so green and lush and supported such a concentration of game that, for our pioneering hunter-gatherer ancestors, who were pushing up from the hard savannah of the Rift Valley, this was the Promised Land. I twisted in the Trappist cell of the aeroplane seat, looked down into the dawn desert. The land of Eden was brown and bare, with ridge after ridge of eroded hillsides. The earth had the withered texture of old skin, the mummified remains of a long-dead body.

To the east the escarpment dropped down serried ranks of brown peaks, a jagged staircase descending to the burning plains of the coast. The Red Sea licked the shore with waves that were hot to the touch.

Five hours after leaving London, the pilot announced that we would soon be arriving. The NO SMOKING sign blinked on and we fastened our seat belts.

As the plane lost height I looked down out of the window. Below were the buildings and roads of Asmara. The colourful little capital had a toyland look about it in the burnt-ochre landscape. As we skimmed down I saw wrecks of MiG fighters and gun emplacements along the runway.

The plane landed with nothing more dangerous than a bump.

There was a hush and a cheer, and a short burst of applause.

The Eritreans did not accompany the touchdown with a charge for the doors, but sat calmly till the plane had taxied to a rest. Many of them had waited half their lifetimes for this moment of return; others had been born in exile. A few more minutes' wait was unimportant.

When the steps had been moved into position the doors opened. The pilot announced that this was Asmara, capital of Free Eritrea, Africa's newest nation, and wished us a pleasant stay.

The people who were flying on to Addis – a mixture of Eritrean exiles and foreign volunteers – looked at us with envy and curiosity as about twenty of us pulled our luggage from the overhead lockers and walked out of the plane. We moved down the aisle of turned faces, and then I stepped out of the door. The airport attendants were already at work, emptying our luggage.

I stood and looked out over the airport buildings. It was a cool morning; the dry barren hillsides stretched away, fading into the cloudless distance. The long dry grass was stroked flat by a gust of breeze. I turned back to the gun emplacements, and the twisted metal of the MiGs.

This was Eritrea.

II

Eritrea was founded by imperial decree on 1 January 1890, by declaration of Umberto I. The Italian influence was obvious from the moment my battered yellow taxi chugged into town.

'It's beautiful,' I said to the taxi driver, an old, grey-fuzzed man who was even older than his car, as I admired the Art Deco capital of the world.

'No new buildings since the nineteen-thirties,' he grumbled through a mouth without teeth. The 1930s were the Fascist period, when investment in the colony, as a base for further expansion, was at its highest. 'Speak Italiano?' the man asked.

'No,' I told him.

'My English very bad.' He turned to look at me and his eyes were very bright under white eyebrows. 'Italiano – good!'

I gave him the name of a hotel as he drove me down deserted streets of neat, whitewashed buildings. Washing hung from the shuttered windows and balconies.

The street signs hadn't been touched up since the pre-war years. They still spoke of the aspirations of the Italian colonists – Bar Diana, Restaurant Milano, Pizza Napoli, Cinema Impero, Bar Royal, Odeon, the Order of the

Cappuccins' cathedral and adjacent nunnery. The main street
was a palm-shaded boulevard that felt like a southern Italian
town. It had had a variety of names over the years. It was now
called Liberation Avenue.

'Italians call it Via Comistato,' the driver told me.

'And the Ethiopians?'

He jammed the car into second gear. 'Haile Selassie
Avenue.'

There were four lanes along Liberation Avenue, along
which a handful of Morris Minors and early Beetles chugged
sedately back and forth like horse-drawn carriages. The street
was dominated by the Gothic tower of the cathedral, and the
bronze angel atop the cupola, cast from Austrian cannon captured in the Great War. Beneath it and the ranks of shuttered
windows the traffic was orderly and quiet. Rush hour
involved about twenty cars. A traffic jam was national news.

The driver indicated with hand signals then took us down
a road of Swiss mansions. I could see how much effort the
Italians had invested in their little African capital. There was
another road of villas, each different to the other, with foun-
tains and statues and bas-reliefs on the walls, and then he
parked with both feet.

'Africa Pensione,' he announced.

I climbed the marble steps; walked past the statue of Caesar
on the front lawn, who gave a magnanimous sweep of his
togaed arm; and pushed through the glass doors.

––––––––––

'We're waiting for the Melotti van,' a waiter told me at the
fifth bar I went into. I hadn't been in Asmara more than two

hours and already I'd found out that the city often ran out of beer. When there was a shortage everyone sat pensively waiting for the Melotti van to arrive. I pulled up a stool at the bar and joined them.

As I sat I conjured up a mental image of the Melotti van: it was something like a wooden cart pulled by shire horses. When it finally did arrive it wasn't far removed, but dated from just this side of the Industrial Revolution. It rattled more than the bottles it carried, and was so encrusted with rust it looked as though it had been hauled out of the sea a week earlier. A sign ran along only one side of the van, which said SIGNOR MELOTTI and then an indecipherable catchphrase in Italian, which had finally succumbed to years of erosion.

Signor Melotti was an Italian who had lived in Massawa before the war. His brewery became a household name in East Africa and Arabia during the war years, when these areas were cut off from European supplies. After he died his factory passed to his daughter. It was said she'd been a supporter of the Eritrean fighters and had been forced to flee to Italy. The factory was confiscated by the Ethiopian government. All that was left now was the family name, the beer and the wheezing old truck.

The beer when it arrived was warm, but the view from my outside seat made the wait worthwhile. I sat and sipped and watched the evening parade along Liberation Avenue, as tall, thin Eritreans in their best clothes did the *passeggiata*, the way their old Italian masters used to do: glamorous young people in immaculate cheap imports, middle-aged men in tweeds, country women in white dresses and shawls. The old gentlemen wore three-piece suits, the young flares, while all the women wore high-waisted Victorian dresses and unbleached

Asmara: Art Deco capital of the world.

cotton shawls. They had gold in their hair and ears, wore heavy Coptic crosses around their necks. There was even a scattering of Sudanese rebel fighters on R&R – tall warriors with tribal scars on their cheeks, whose giant loping strides contrasted strongly with the Eritreans' upright and elegant carriage.

After my beer it was already late, or late as far as Asmara was concerned, where everyone was at home by nine-thirty. I walked back to my hotel down Liberation Avenue, into Peace Avenue, and along Via L. da Vinci, and found out one of the reasons why Asmara was the safest capital in the world. A gang of men wielding long truncheons and wearing trenchcoats and black balaclavas passed me going in the opposite direction. They were out-of-work fighters who made up the police. A few metres down the road they administered summary justice to a pair of drunks, who may or may not have been unstable before, but who certainly couldn't walk afterwards.

The next morning at the hotel I mentioned this episode to the owner's daughter, a girl called Aster who spoke English with a shy smile.

'Yes,' she replied, 'but under the Ethiopians, people were shot.'

———

Aster had been born in Sudan, where her family had fled during the war. Her family had brought her back to Eritrea after liberation. She was proud of her country, and proud of her capital.

'Asmara's much safer than other African cities,' Aster told me. 'Eritrea is different from the rest of Africa,' she insisted.

'We're going to have a different future to the other African countries. Eritrea will be like Singapore or Taiwan.'

The language spoken in Asmara is Tigrinya, the name of the majority group and lingua franca of much of Eritrea. Tigrinya is a Semitic language. Here links with the Jews run deep, even into pre-history. The tribes of the Ethiopian highlands claim descent from Ethiopic, grandson of Noah. Their greatest ruler was the legendary Queen Makeda.

Her story is told in the Kebra Nagast, The Glory of Kings, fortieth book of the Old Testament. Lost for centuries, it was first translated into Spanish in 1528, and subsequently suppressed by European scholars because it contained a triple heresy: that the Ark of the Covenant had been taken and treasured for centuries in Africa; that the emperors of Ethiopia were descended from King Solomon; and, most controversially, that God's chosen people were black.

Queen Makeda lived in the eleventh and tenth centuries BC, owned a fleet of seventy-three ships, and sponsored caravans of over five hundred camels that traded as far afield as Palestine and India. Her seat of power was Sabea, from which she ruled modern-day northern Ethiopia, Eritrea and Yemen – the area that is known in the Bible as the Land of Kush. Her people worshipped the sun, king of the gods, and a pantheon of other deities of tree, water and stone; they raised up images of gold and silver to worship. It was a kingdom famous for its gold and incense, and the African trade of slaves and ivory that it controlled. But it is through the name of her capital that Queen Makeda is known to us: the Queen of Sabea, or, as she is now called, the Queen of Sheba.

When King Solomon decided he was going to build a

temple to the Lord, he sent messages abroad for merchants of the world to bring him all that he required to make his structure worthy of God's house. Rumours of his wisdom and wealth spread. The young Queen Makeda decided to go and learn kingship from him.

It must have been a fantastical BC meeting in the Jerusalem palace of Solomon: the beautiful, gold-laden black Queen, tall and slender with severe cheekbones and icon-round eyes; and the energetic and gifted Jewish King. The man of limitless energy who built Israel and exercised his energy on his seven hundred wives.

She presented him with gifts; he showed her the building site of his temple. Like Peter the Great, he was king and artisan combined. He personally jumped in where necessary with hammer or chisel, checking the stonemasons' angles, then wiping his hands clean. They spent long hours together discussing the problems of kingship, and philosophies on ruling. She was entranced by his voice, and he by her foreign beauty. His learning amazed her, and during her stay he converted her to the worship of Yahweh, the One God. After six months the Queen told him of her desire to return home. The King sat and tried to think how to seduce her before she left; invited her for a meal alone together.

In the tangle of purple hangings and carpets, aglow in the lamplight, sparkling with marble and the treacherous wink of precious stones, the young Queen sat for the meal of which she was dessert. The King burned aromatic powders, scattering oil of myrrh and frankincense into the air. He fed Makeda with sweetmeats and salted fish, and drinks of watered-down wine. When the attendants left them alone Solomon tricked the young Queen; raped her in the cave of candlelight.

I am black, but comely, O ye daughters of Jerusalem:
    the king hath brought me into his chambers:
His left hand is under my head, and his right hand
    doth embrace me.
My beloved is white and ruddy, the chiefest among
    ten thousand.
His head is as the most fine gold, his locks are bushy,
    and black as a raven.
His hands are as gold rings set with the beryl: his
    belly is as bright ivory overset with sapphires.
His legs are as pillars of marble, set upon sockets of
    fine gold.
Let him kiss me with the kisses of his mouth; his
    mouth is most sweet.

The son of the Queen of Sheba and King Solomon founded the dynasty of Solomaic kings that ruled Axum until the tenth century AD. The Axumite Empire was described by the third-century Persian writer Manni as one of the four great kingdoms in the world, with Persia, Rome and China. It had well-recorded links to the Hellenistic world, India and Rome (twice repelling the legionaries). It was the only African civilisation apart from Egypt to have such tangible links to the Ancient World, and raised the highest obelisks ever seen (thirty-three metres).

The Axumite Empire lasted, at the height of its power, from the first century AD until the seventh, when the silting-up of its ports and the rise of Islam in Arabia cut the Axumites off from the rest of the Christian world. But even then the Axumites did not die out. They resisted the invasion of Islam,

Palace ruins from the Axumite Empire.

whose armies pushed as far as Spain and India, and moved
the area of their control inland to the south and west. The tradition of Solomaic kings continued, in a debased form,
throughout the Ethiopian Dark Ages.

The Axumite peoples, once unified, separated into the
ethnic groups that now make up the Muslim and Christian
peoples of Ethiopia and Eritrea: the Amhara, Tigrinya and
Tigre. The ancient language of Ge'ez remained the language
of the Church, but split into the modern languages of the
area, just as Latin became French, Portuguese, Spanish and
Italian in Europe. The Ge'ez script itself, a syllabic alphabet
where each consonant has eight variations according to the
vowel that accompanies it, is shared by two very different
areas of the world: Armenia in Central Asia and the Ethiopian

area of Africa. The reason for this is that both Armenia and Ethiopia were converted to Christianity at around the same time in history by Syrian missionaries.

Cut off from the Christian world by the rise of Islam, Axum faded from knowledge into legend. As Gibbon wrote, the Ethiopians were 'forgetful of the world, by whom they were forgotten'.

And still the Axumite Empire remains almost completely unknown. There are histories of Africa that do not mention it at all.

———————

Aster began teaching me Tigrinya. As she and I studied, every so often we came across words that had been borrowed from other languages and reincarnated into Tigrinya. As I began to recognise them it was like unpeeling layers of history.

The earliest borrowings were from Arabic, whose speakers came as middlemen to run the Ottoman and later the Egyptian Empire. The area of highland Eritrea was their far-thest-flung province, a hard and hostile post, a long way from the cool tiled interiors of the Levant. They were not gentle rulers. The Tigrinya still call an impossible situation 'Turks' rule'. Arabic loan-words were used to insult other people, to give orders. It was the language of ruler to slave.

The easiest words to learn came from the Italians. The Italians introduced the Eritrean peoples to the modern world; equipped them with the necessary language. The Tigrinya borrowed words from Italian for everything modern: car, machine, carrot, café, *latteria*, pasta. After five minutes of talking about food I felt half fluent in Tigrinya already.

The Italians ruled Eritrea until 1941, when the British drove the Fascist regime out of East Africa and then governed for ten years under UN mandate. English words were sprinkled ostentatiously in speech as if they were an exotic spice. But the English words weren't borrowed from the time of the British, but from the influx of consumerism and television: deadline, allergy, moderate, battery, Colgate.

I asked Aster if there were any Amharic loan-words, from the Ethiopians.

'None,' she said. 'The Ethiopians had nothing to teach us.'

The next morning I went to a café to get breakfast. It was called the American Bar, and inside the decor was still James Dean, lino and chrome. It dated from the time when Asmara was the Saigon of Africa, with strip bars, beer and too many GIs. But the welcome was very un-American. The locals turned to stare and the cappuccino machine hissed.

I scattered a few *salamat*s (hellos), but everyone stared as if I was mad. I began to think I was. One old man raised steel-grey eyebrows and said, '*Buon giorno. Va bene?*'

'*Bella*,' I replied.

He nodded in satisfaction then buried his head in the V of his newspaper.

I sat down; the men watched me just to make sure. We sat uneasily and the waiter hung around like a traffic warden. I ordered a cappuccino, and sat and sipped nervously. It was the genuine article. The waiter hovered around and rushed to help me pour in a dose of sugar, stirred the cup for me too.

'Anything else?' he asked.

'What have you got?'

He offered me ice-cream.

'Ice-cream for breakfast?'

He gasped. Yes.

There were three flavours: blue, green and brown. I chose brown. The waiter brought it across the room and put it in front of me. It melted into the white bowl. He waited for my reaction with a hopeful smile. I took a spoonful, licked and nodded. It tasted more like blue.

'*Bella!*' I announced, and his face split into a grateful smile.

As I walked around Asmara, the whole city felt as if the modern age had never arrived. Everything dated from the 1950s, the golden age of Eritrea, when Asmara was the most industrialised part of Africa. Its factories were exporting manufactured goods and tinned fruit all over the world, there were trade unions and political parties, schooling for the growing urban population and an educated middle class. But war had pickled the city; after forty years it was preserved and wrinkled and strange.

Bar Impero felt the same as the American Bar. There was a polished lino floor, and lots of chrome-plated tubular furniture doing life. There were archaic 50s-style ashtrays; a sign on the wall said MELOTTI'S BEER – SUPERIOR QUALITY.

There were a few old men in brown suits sitting reading newspapers. They had come in as youngsters and never left. A few waiters in white doctors' coats served them their hourly medicine of coffee and cake.

The only concession to the modern world was a faded Ethiopian Tourist Board poster on one wall which claimed that the weather included 'Four Seasons in One Day', while another picture showed a squad of Eritrean fighters in skin-tight shorts and great legs planting their red, green and blue flag on the top of a hill.

I sat and ordered a cappuccino.

After half an hour I ordered another.

And another.

And then I needed the toilet.

That night back at the Africa Pensione I had a shower. The red tap was cold and the blue tap was cold as well. I shaved in a sink where a family of cockroaches were having a bath and then retired to my room.

Instead of fighting for independence, I began to suspect that the Eritreans had spent the last thirty years sipping coffee, confusing foreigners and eating blue ice-cream for breakfast. The stories I'd read about the years of war just didn't seem to correlate. Maybe I'd landed in the wrong Eritrea.

The next morning I found a sign in a shop window along Liberation Avenue which proved there had been a war after all.

It said: WELCOME TO FREE ERITREA.

———————

Awot was six foot across, had eyes that laughed, and laughter that shook the ground. He moved through rooms like a social earthquake.

Awot had been born into a world which was a house of horrors – a Hollywood action thriller where violence reached out, off the television screen and sucked you in. Where the people being shot were your friends and family. Where the charred bodies on the news leant out of the television and kissed you goodbye. An interactive terror, except that you weren't even interactive, you were the powerless victim. Awot grew up in such a world, grew up with pain as a fact of everyday life – and came out laughing.

I said I was in awe.

'Do you know why I am so happy?' he grinned. 'It's because I never expected to live through the war. Every day I am still alive is a bonus.'

Awot had grown up in the south of Eritrea. His father and three uncles all lived in the same house. They treated each other's children as their own. When they played in the yard Awot forgot who were his brothers and sisters and who were his cousins. It wasn't important. His father had been an askari soldier in the Italian forces. His duties were, until the 1930s, mainly confined to suppression of *shifta* bandits, but with the rise of the Fascists the colony of Eritrea changed.

The Fascist years saw a tremendous expansion in Eritrea as it was geared up for the Italian invasion of Ethiopia. By 1929 Massawa was the largest port on the east coast of Africa, bigger than Mombasa or Dar es Salaam. The road network was expanded, and military recruitment doubled. In 1935 Awot's father joined in the invasion of Abyssinia, and the money he earned allowed him to move his family to Asmara. The Fascist regime had imposed a kind of apartheid of its own on the colony: natives were not allowed to walk down Liberation Avenue, or to use the same churches as whites, so Awot's father moved to the native areas, and built a small house.

Times changed when the British invaded from Sudan.

In early 1940 all Europe had fallen to the Blitzkrieg. America was neutral; Stalin was at an uneasy truce with

Hitler; and, all alone, Britain held the breach. Besieged by U-boats and the masses of the Luftwaffe, the situation looked worse than bleak. Even the Channel Islands, oldest overseas possessions of the Crown, were surrendered to the Germans without a fight. The Empire was facing its hour of reckoning. At the head of her armies stood Winston Churchill. He set to work mobilising all the Empire's resources against Nazism, and delivered earth-shaking speeches: 'If the British Empire and its Commonwealth last for a thousand years, men will say, "This was their finest hour!"' he defiantly announced. 'I have not become the First Minister of the Crown in order to preside over the liquidation of the British Empire!'

But the Italians and Japanese had other ideas. Japan wanted to head a Greater East Asia Co-Prosperity Sphere. She was setting out to swallow all the eastern Empire, from Hong Kong to India, with New Zealand and Australia as well. Mussolini set his claim on Malta and Cyprus, Egypt, East Africa as far as the equator, Iraq and Sudan. Although the Japanese soldiers were marching unhindered through Asia, it was this Italian threat that was taken more seriously, because from their colonies in Ethiopia and Eritrea they could attack Egypt and take the Suez Canal, the very lifeline of the Empire.

The importance attached to this waterway is illustrated by the fact that, before the war, the only British standing expeditionary force was designed to go, not to France, but to Egypt. At the most critical moment of the Battle of Britain, when an invasion of Britain seemed imminent, Churchill sent a hundred aircraft and an armoured brigade to the eastern Mediterranean. Control Egypt and you could control the Suez Canal, the jugular of the Raj and the Empire as a whole. On that narrow piece of water depended all the oil supplies, the links with India. Whatever else happened, Egypt must not fall. It was in defence of Egypt that the first African battles of the Second World War were fought, not against Rommel in the Sahara, but against the Italians over the colony of Eritrea.

At first the odds were ridiculously stacked against the Empire. The British-led government of Sudan had 2500 men, mostly belonging to the locally recruited Sudanese Defence Force, whose badge was an Arabic warrior mounted on a camel. The Italians had 250,000, with two hundred aircraft and many tanks. But they were a conscript army: uneasy. Isolated.

Despite this massive advantage the Italians ruinously over-estimated the strength of the British. They staged a tentative assault on the border post of Kassala, manned by less than a hundred men, in July 1940, then retreated and waited for revenge.

By September the Italians had lost the initiative. Britain brought in reinforcements from Kenya, South Africa and India. General Platt was granted command and moved into Eritrea in early 1941, capturing the border town of Tessenei then moving on, as the EPLF did much later, to take Agordat and Keren.

It was the battle for Keren that was the crux of the World War II campaign. The town lies at the strategic heart of Eritrea, and commands the pass from which the land rises up to the highlands, taking you out of the sun-baked plains below to the mountain valleys above. It was at this gorge that the Italians made their last defence. The road was so narrow that only one car could drive along at a time. The Italians

blocked it with masonry, dug connecting trenches and decorated the overhanging peaks with barbed wire.

There was a month of fighting before the British forced
the Italian position. Generale Lorenzini was killed in the fighting. The pursuit was a rout. Eritrea fell when Asmara
surrendered on April Fool's Day, 1941.

The speed of their success, against such high odds, left the
British over-stretched, and so the colony was run by local
Italians supervised by a few British officers for the rest of the
war. The British continued to rule Eritrea after the war under a
UN mandate. They removed the colour bar and fostered education at elementary level, encouraged industrial organisation
and civil participation in government, but when the mandate
ran out in 1950 they took away $86 million worth of infra-
structure, including Massawa's dry docks, canning plant and
cement factory, as 'reparations' against the Italian government.

The British had always regarded Eritrea as an unnatural
creation. They wanted the country to be split: the Muslim
areas going to their colony of Sudan and the Christian areas
to Haile Selassie, King of Kings, Conquering Lion of the Tribe
of Judah, Emperor of Ethiopia. The Italians wanted their
colony back. But it was clear that times had changed: the
world was no longer an extension of European *realpolitik*. A
UN delegation was appointed to decide.

After a brief visit, delegates from Pakistan, Burma,
Norway, Guatemala and South Africa came to various con-
clusions. Burma and South Africa recommended a close
federation of Eritrea and Ethiopia. Pakistan and Guatemala
called for a ten-year trusteeship followed by full independence. But the Korean War of 1950 meant that Eritrea would
get none of these options.

Emperor Haile Selassie, King of Kings, Conquering Lion of the Tribe of Judah; and last of the line of Abyssinian kings.

Haile Selassie was a staunch ally of the West in the vital area of the Red Sea and Suez Canal. He sent troops from his Imperial Bodyguard to fight alongside the Americans in Korea. In the political climate of the times, when countries were falling to communism and socialism, the support of a black leader of a developing country was a major moral boost to the Americans. In return for his help, the US supported Haile Selassie's claims on Eritrea.

John Foster Dulles, the then US Secretary of State, told the UN General Assembly that, although the wishes of the Eritrean people must be taken into account, 'The strategic interests of the United States in the Red Sea basin make it necessary that the country is linked to our ally Ethiopia.'

His strategic interests caused the longest-running war of the twentieth century.

The longest war in African history.

On 2 December 1950, resolution 390A(v) made Eritrea, the most advanced part of sub-Saharan Africa, with mature political parties and independent labour unions – a feudal kingdom that had escaped colonisation during the Scramble for Africa by joining in the scramble itself – an autonomous unit federated to Ethiopia. While the rest of Africa was gaining its independence, the Eritreans found themselves with new colonisers – the Ethiopians.

It struck no one in the UN as strange that the integrity of the democratically elected Eritrean assembly would be guaranteed by an absolute monarch whose mind was in the realm of the divine right of kings.

Haile Selassie was the Emperor of Ethiopia, and inspiration for the Rastafarian religion, which took its name from his

pre-coronation name: Ras Tafari. Symbol of black freedom
across the world, Haile Selassie is famous for his speech to the
UN protesting against the Italian invasion of Ethiopia in
1936: talking of freedom and the rights of people to live
without foreign oppression and aggression. But when he was
given Eritrea he treated the people there the way earlier
Abyssinian warlords had done their newly conquered lands,
and divided it up between his feudal chiefs.

His son-in-law was made Governor. He banned the use of
Arabic or Tigrinya in schools. All books not written in the
ruling tribe's Amhara language were burnt. Eritrea's economic
dominance in Ethiopia was undermined by closure of industries and transferral of others to Ethiopia proper. Protests
were matched with ever-increasing brutality. There was a general strike, and the subsequent police massacre went
unnoticed by the international community.

In March 1958, 550 people were killed or injured by
Ethiopian soldiers repressing a strike. Since the UN had written the federal constitution of Eritrea, and was the guarantor
of Eritrean rights, the Eritreans tried to raise the matter with
the UN. But the UN wouldn't even let them inside the assembly to state their case. As far as the world was concerned
Eritrea no longer existed.

When, in 1962, Haile Selassie finally abolished the Eritrean
Parliament by royal decree, no one cared.

On 1 September 1961 a man called Hammed Idris Awate
attacked a police post in Agordat and captured sixteen guns.
The first shots of the revolution had been fired.

This was the time of Vietnam: Mai Lai, Agent Orange and B-52 carpet bombings. The US trained the Ethiopian military in counter-insurgency techniques; techniques they had used in Nam. Techniques so brutal they caused the first mass exodus of Eritrean civilians to the Sudan.

There were two groups fighting the war against the Ethiopians. The members of the ELF (Eritrean Liberation Front), the larger of the two groups, were predominantly Muslim, and allied to the traditional landlords. Journalists who visited the front said they were easygoing, fun to be with. They joked and swore, and loved their guns. When they arrived in a village they acted like the traditional *shifta* bandits, demanding food and coffee from the locals. Sometimes they paid and sometimes they didn't.

The EPLF (Eritrean People's Liberation Front) were very different. An offshoot of the ELF, their leaders had been smuggled into Maoist China during the death throes of the Cultural Revolution. There they studied the thoughts of Mao, whose tenet was that 'Social revolution is integral to political revolution,' that social reform was part of the resistance struggle.

The EPLF educated their fighters, taught them world politics, explained why no one cared about the Eritreans. They had a unified set of beliefs and values. The journalists described the EPLF fighters as serious and earnest, stiff in company; not people you would warm to easily.

They were confrontational towards Westerners about their respective governments' policies. Confrontational about the fact that the world ignored their struggle. They wanted to know why the UN, guarantor of their rights, refused to even listen to their pleas.

The EPLF's fighters followed Mao's dictums for guerrillas. They were taught not to take anything from the people without paying for it. When they moved through communities, they were like fish in water. When they conquered new territory, the fighters came first, to protect the villagers. They gained the affection and trust of the people. Then they started to educate them.

As peasants anywhere, the people thought of themselves and their families first and foremost, stuck to their traditions, to their livestock and land. They only listened because everything they cared about was threatened by the war. At the beginning men and women were gathered separately, to listen to what the EPLF cadres had to say. The message was that the people must stop thinking of themselves as separated by religion, race, tribe or sex.

I once saw a documentary following two female fighters who went to a newly liberated village to try to persuade the people there that men and women were equal.

The elders of the village gathered to discuss this concept of equality that the two fighters had dropped on their doorstep. They held the idea of sexual equality up before their eyes, and turned it in the light like a curious instrument. They had never heard of such a thing before. They took a long look and decided they definitely did not like it. All the villagers gathered together, men and women, and argued against it. They reeled off the lore of their ancestors, the laws of the Bible and the Koran – prejudice in its most legitimate form.

When the fighters talked back the village elders listened, stony-faced. The women villagers sat apart and giggled. Then the fighters began to counter the arguments one by one. The fighters never raised their voices, even to the most stupid of arguments. They listened and then argued back, using the more enlightened parts of the Bible and the Koran as their evidence. They discussed for a week. At the end the villagers relented: they would discuss this thing called 'Equality'.

EPLF workers continued to implement social reform as they fought the Ethiopians. They taught the different racial groups to think of themselves as Eritreans. There was land reform, and village committees. There were men's associations and women's associations. They would divide into groups of 'poor', 'middle' and 'rich', each of which would have a representative to sit in a village congress.

When there were murmurs in the crowd, the fighters patiently explained that the members of the associations would be introduced to new farming methods, they would receive low-cost goods, and that a mill would be set up to save the women the job of hand-grinding flour.

There were more problems trying to mobilise the women. They had never been given a role in running even domestic life. The society was ultra conservative, on both sides of the sexual divide. When meetings to mobilise the women were called, the opposition from husbands was strong, but the women's personal inhibitions also hindered any progress. Eventually, with time, the women's movement grew. The women were taught the words they needed to understand their oppressed role within society. With the right vocab they began to express themselves, to talk about their position in the world and how to improve it.

Under the new system there was a modest redistribution of land from the feudal landlords. Village militias were set up, with more land reform, and a strengthening of ties with the EPLF as the people's trust and reliance grew. Local schooling was introduced, and free healthcare, and of course protection from the Ethiopians.

The fighters of the EPLF told the nomads that Eritrea was a rich country of gold and oil and nickel and gas. If only they could be free then life would be a utopia of milk and honey, and battery-operated radios. When they were free then everyone would have lots of goats, butter, meat and coffee. The exploited had to fight the exploiters and then a socialist paradise would await them. And the people believed them.

In 1974, weakened by the war in Eritrea and famine at home, Haile Selassie's arthritic regime was overthrown by a clique of military officers. A committee called the Dergue was established. They promised change from his outdated feudal kingdom. With their socialist agenda they won the support of the Marxist EPLF and ELF, and all the other Ethiopians who wanted to modernise their country. As a symbolic gesture of reconciliation the Dergue appointed an Eritrean, General Aman, as their leader. But the repression continued and after General Aman resigned in protest the Dergue placed him under house arrest and had him shot.

One of the next victims was Emperor Haile Selassie himself. He was driven unceremoniously out of his palace in a Volkswagen Beetle. Three thousand years of Solomaic rule: men who claimed descent from King Solomon and the young Queen of Sheba ended when he was bundled into a safe house and shot. Next to die was the soldier who'd been detailed to kill him.

In the whirlpool of revolution the losers were sucked down, while a ferocious few defied the laws of decency and skimmed to the top. There was nothing some people wouldn't do to stay afloat. Two prime ministers and fifty-five other high-ranking officials followed the Emperor, executed without trial. Thousands upon thousands followed them, in a mounting pile of corpses and paperwork, as the families of the unfortunate were billed for the cost of the execution.

The Dergue responded to public protests and continued revolution in Eritrea with mass arrests and executions. The Ethiopian revolution turned on itself in a ferocious purge. The spiral of extreme violence ended in February 1976 with the execution of seven party leaders, including the nominal head of the Dergue.

From the bloody dream of revolution, Mengistu Haile Mariam – the bastard son of an Amharic warrior – woke as leader.

Born in 1937, he had been an army officer before the coup. Now he was the President, with the sole virtue of having murdered all his competitors.

Mengistu's government was so ponderously top-heavy, with four vice-presidents, one prime minister, five deputy prime ministers and forty ministers, that he was the only person who could get anything done. And the first thing he did after seizing control was to send delegations to places like Tanzania, China and India in search of an ideology.

The country that impressed him most was North Korea. During his visit to Pyongyang he decided that Marxism was the future. He wanted the carefully primed, choreographed crowds who clapped, cheered and cursed on order.

While Haile Selassie was emperor, there had been sympathetic stories about the Eritrean struggle in the pages of leftist journals all over the world. But Mengistu's conversion cut off any hope the Eritreans had of getting outside support. The

Lt-Col Mengistu Haile Mariam, Chairman of the Dergue,
in a rare press conference.

Western powers would never support a Communist rebel movement; and the Soviets had no interest in supporting Communist
rebels fighting against a Communist government. People who
had once been supporters now rubbished the Eritreans. Fidel
Castro declared that although the Eritrean movement had
once been progressive, it had now come under the control of
reactionary states such as Sudan and Saudi Arabia.

For the entire thirty-year struggle the Eritrean people
remained unsupported. They never received outside help.

Mengistu's disembodied policies pitched Ethiopia into a
decade and a half of established disorder. It was a simple
retelling of the very old story of Power and the Corrupted.

Because the Bolsheviks had faced fourteen hostile countries after the Russian Revolution, Mengistu fantasised a list of fourteen enemies of Ethiopia. He wrote his own Red Book, which was green. He had a gold-plated chair, and sat upon it with the regal demeanour of a hyena. He led the fashion in designer suits imported from Europe; drank the finest wines and whiskies; put the whole country through a nightmare of his own delusion.

In meetings of the OAU (Organisation of African Unity) he rubbed shoulders with the likes of Idi Amin, President Mobutu of Zaire and Hastings Banda. They were a club of mafia bosses, running a whole continent and ruining the lives of millions. They embezzled, and massacred, and destroyed with impunity. And the rest of the world only took an interest if it was in their interests.

———————

In 1974 the population of Asmara was 200,000. In 1977 it was less than 90,000. Terror, murder and war had caused a third of the country's population to flee into exile. A million people were rotting in Sudanese refugee camps. Yet despite the suffering, the Eritreans were winning the war.

By 1977 90 per cent of Eritrea was in the hands of the EPLF and ELF. Victory waited just beyond the next offensive. To prevent the break-up of their new satellite, the Communist allies poured in massive aid. In six months the equivalent of US$1000 million of military aid arrived from the Eastern Bloc as tanks, guns, war-planes, ammunition and troops.

The North Koreans trained Sparta brigades to help fight the Eritrean rebels: raving bands of kung-fu-kicking and knife-throwing Ethiopian tribesmen. Cuban troops, the descendants of freed slaves, volunteered to protect their African homeland from capitalism and American imperialism. Soviet warships bombarded the rebel positions. Cuban and Yemeni troops joined in the front-line fighting.

The ELF tried to protect the villages and people they had liberated. The Soviet assault smashed them. The EPLF followed the example of Mao and the Long March, and retreated to the rugged north of the country. They consolidated their position in the hills of the north around Nakfa, and prepared for the onslaught.

During this time Awot was a pupil at the Cistercian monastery in Decamhare, a small town south of Asmara on the road to Ethiopia. The school was safe; the war stayed outside its doors. Brother Yosuf, the abbot, was a grey-topped old man with a dribble and a stutter. He made the boys spend their spare hours in physical labour, their weekends working on the farm, and when they went to bed he made them sleep in their clothes because he said a good Christian should always be ready to work for God.

Brother Yosuf explained to the students how his personal code of physical discomfort had brought him closer to God and would bring them closer too. They had to be very patient because Brother Yosuf stuttered so much, which made them snigger. But when Brother Yosuf stuttered over the readings from the Old Testament the boys didn't laugh. When God destroyed the cities of Sodom and Gomorrah, or killed the first-born of each Egyptian family, then this was a ruler they could understand.

'Somehow I began to lose my belief that what was happening

to Eritrea could be stopped if we all prayed to God,' Awot told me with a smile. 'It seemed that what was happening was because of God's will. There was nothing we could do but fight.'

The EPLF fighters dug hundreds of miles of trenches and underground factories. They created the longest hospital in the world, excavated along an entire hillside. They held their meetings under the shade of trees, and had classrooms under overhanging rocks where the MiG fighters couldn't see them. As the Ethiopian and Soviet generals wound up their first big swing the EPLF fighters waited in caves and underground chambers for the Soviet sledgehammer. It was a hammer that over the next decade would hit them very often and very, very hard. The Battle of Nakfa, the mountain stronghold of the EPLF, was the biggest battle of the war.

It did not last weeks or months, but thirteen years.

The first assault was in July 1978, when the Eritreans retreated before Yemeni- and Cuban-spearheaded campaigns. The second was in November 1978, targeting urban strongholds like Keren. When it fell Mengistu triumphantly declared it 'the end of the seventeen-year-old separatist dream'. The last Ethiopian prize was the stronghold of Nakfa.

They attacked it in January and February 1979. And again in April. In July 1979 they attacked a fifth time. While the official media were trumpeting success after success, each broke like waves upon cliffs of steel. The rebels were dismissed as 'Arab invaders from the north', but the Ethiopians were even struggling with the control of the capital. On a visit to Asmara, Mengistu was injured in a daring EPLF attack at the airport.

As he recovered from his wounds, cancelling speeches across the country, Mengistu began to obsess about this troublesome province. Eritrea dominated his life so much that in the end he spent three-quarters of the country's budget on the war. Lives were as nothing to Mengistu's personal obsession to crush the Eritrean people. Even during the Ethiopian famine of 1984, when Live Aid was raising millions of pounds of relief, food aid landing on the dockside of ports like Massawa and Assab was loaded straight on to Soviet ships in return for more weapons.

At first the Ethiopian troops were told they were on bandit-extermination campaigns. They entered Eritrea like conquerors: a hundred thousand peasants banded together into a massive feudal war party. They took only a few days' rations with them; the rest they were to get by pillaging the local population. They brandished their teeth and swords, and bragged to each other how they would slaughter the Eritrean bandits. Their orders were to kill anyone they met. Mengistu told them in a speech to 'leave a path of devastation behind you to show the way to others following behind you ... to seize the Eritrean women, and sire Ethiopian children'.

The men in the Peasants' March had no idea that the bandits they were facing were experienced soldiers of the twentieth century, armed with corresponding weaponry. As they indulged in rape and slaughter the rebels moved silently in. The Ethiopians' shields and swords were no use against Kalashnikovs. They were ambushed and wiped out. Over twenty thousand of them died.

The Ethiopian official media reported the crushing of the Eritrean rebels. Despite the continued fighting, radio and papers declared that 'In Eritrea peace, prosperity and optimism prevail.'

With each success the reputation of the EPLF fighters grew and spread throughout the places where there were Eritrean people – in Eritrea itself, in Europe, North America and the Middle East. From villages all over Eritrea young men and women walked to the liberated areas. Fighters of the various ELF groups went over to join the EPLF. Eritrean students left their American or European schools and colleges, and returned to fight.

Mengistu waited until 1982 to launch his really big attack – the Sixth Offensive. It had started as a cultural festival to try to charm the Eritrean people and show them the benefits of life in Soviet Ethiopia. There were festivals and Soviet-style dance and music events planned. Mengistu was sure that Eritrean resistance would collapse once they had been organised into the Workers' Party of Ethiopia. But as the weeks progressed he decided to ditch the cultural element, and just make it the biggest military offensive of the war: 'to end once and for all the organised banditry'.

After a month-long build-up Mengistu threw a hundred thousand Ethiopian troops into battle. The weapons included helicopter gunships, colossal Antonov bombers and toxic gas. This time the Ethiopian troops were not peasants but the country's well-educated university and high-school graduates. Their education was a prerequisite so that they could read the technical instructions on the Russian weaponry.

It was the largest attack the EPLF had had to endure, and, apart from the shifting desert war between Rommel and Montgomery, the biggest military offensive ever mounted in Africa. In poured brigade after brigade of Ethiopia's educated youth: future teachers, administrators, doctors, businessmen –

the elite of the young people of Ethiopia. They died in their thousands. It was the Ethiopian Somme.

And yet, despite the terrible casualties, the Ethiopians began to capture the EPLF trenches, one by one.

When they were on the edge of capturing Nakfa the Ethiopian Chief of Staff ordered a halt so that Mengistu's favourite 3rd Infantry could have the honour of winning the battle. There was a delay as they were brought forward, and by the time they arrived it was too late. They attacked and were driven back by regrouping EPLF soldiers.

Mengistu's last offensive came in 1983, with no fanfare. It was called the Silent Offensive because there was no announcement in the media. It was led by a Soviet field marshal.

The EPLF were taken by surprise, and Ethiopian troops pushed up into the lowlands. They nearly succeeded in surrounding the EPLF in Nakfa, but again were pushed back. The attack ground to a halt, and acrimony resulted. The Russians blamed the Ethiopians, and the Ethiopians blamed the Russians.

And then there was famine.

In 1984, the worst year of the Ethiopian famine, Mengistu was concentrating solely on preparations for the tenth anniversary of his revolution. That the rains had failed three times in the north of Ethiopia was of no concern to him. While North Korean workmen were busy decorating the streets of Addis Ababa with garlands, the police were guarding the roads into the city, stopping the starving people from spoiling the party. To say that people were dying of hunger in a socialist paradise was to be an enemy of the state. Humanitarian workers were silenced. A handful of ministers were taken on a drive through the countryside north of Addis. Their limousine was scratched by thickets of imploring hands. But still no one dared speak out.

At last one man, Dawit Giorgis, the head of the Ethiopian Relief Commission, put his life on the line and appealed directly to the international press. The famine became the news story of the decade. The world looked into the starving face of Ethiopia and froze. Mengistu denied there was a famine. When denial was no longer possible he blamed the disaster on CIA spies.

During the whole terrible year Mengistu spent only twenty-five minutes at a relief centre. Cholera swept through the capital. Bureaucracy held up food in the ports, where it rotted. Military hardware was given priority; other food aid went to the USSR in return for more arms.

Finally Mengistu used the famine against his enemies. Relief was cut off to suspect populations. Feeding stations were burnt, the people herded out into the withered land.

Attacks on relief stations were blamed on the rebels.

Then Mengistu decided that the war against the rebels was going badly because all the relief was dampening the military ardour of his people. Giving his people food for free was making them too soft. He cut off aid.

———————

'In the summer of 1987 I started work as an informant for the EPLF,' Awot said, taking a swig of Melotti. 'I had always been interested in liberation when I was a student, but it was too dangerous to get involved then. When I graduated from Addis Ababa University I returned to Eritrea and joined straight away. A fellow-conspirator in my cell was arrested and so I decided to flee. I only had as long to escape as the torturers took to find out my name.'

The day after his friend's disappearance Awot took a long walk out to the next village and never returned. The next day the secret police shot five bullets through his door and broke into his abandoned room. The same evening the tortured body of Awot's fellow-conspirator was dumped in the street, and the women of the village, in their white shawls of cotton, wailed loudly as they gathered up his corpse and took it home for the last time.

The mother and sisters of the dead man wailed to see their loved one's blood-streaked face, and the women of the village screeched their grief and anger – but there was a practised note in their grief. This kind of thing happened so often.

Awot found that there were 160 other men and women joining up to fight Mengistu's regime. They walked at night and hid from aircraft patrols during the day. To reach EPLF-held areas they had to cross through Ethiopian territory.

'The most dangerous moment,' he told me, 'came when we had to pass under a bridge on the main Asmara–Addis road. As we crossed under the Italian girder bridge Ethiopian soldiers discovered us and they started shooting.

'None of the EPLF was even hit. The Ethiopian conscripts were so frightened they just shot wildly into the dark,' Awot said, and his eyes were wide as he relived it in his mind.

The group kept moving for two days solid, until their guides were sure that they had evaded the enemy. They rested for three days as MiG fighters searched for them. Then at last, after a month of walking, they arrived in the now legendary mountain fortress of Nakfa.

————

Awot took me to his house in Asmara to introduce me to some fighters he knew. 'There's a difference between reading about something in a book and meeting the people who were there,' he told me.

We walked out of central Asmara to a place called DenDen. Awot's house was a single-storey building set in a large walled compound. The yard walls were painted a pale dawn-blue. I sat on a wooden stool and enjoyed the fresh afternoon air. Awot gave me a wallet of photographs to look at. I thumbed through them. A friend of his came and she sat down while he went to make tea.

The photos were all of 'the Field'. There were many shots of groups of fighters – dirty but determined revolutionaries who sat in groups and posed for the camera. All the fighters looked youthful, even the old. They had the ragged young look of Che Guevara. They sat under trees, under patchwork tarpaulin camouflage mottled with sunlight, or in clean, white-painted rooms. Although their faces were different, somehow they all looked the same: long afro hair, identical shining eyes, dark skin and white smiles.

'You all looked very happy in the Field,' I said to the woman.

I could tell that she'd been a fighter because she still looked like the people in the photos. Seven years of freedom couldn't undo the look of confidence, and her hands still followed the deliberate movements of a soldier cleaning a gun or pulling the trigger.

Her name was Senait.

Senait was tall and thin with dreadlocks wrapped around her skull like snakes around the head of Medusa. She crouched with her long legs under her, and silently clapped her hands again and again.

Elated EPLF soldiers on captured Soviet amphibious vehicle.

When I spoke she looked at me and shrugged. 'We were much happier than now. We were young, we did not think about our lives. We only ate and slept, and prepared ourselves for dying in the struggle. I was in the Field for eighteen years. I sometimes wonder where those eighteen years went. We did not worry about anything. We had one set of clothes and that was enough.'

Awot came out with the tea, which brimmed over and spilt over the tray. He passed round the cups, which we slurped contemplatively. Another friend of his came, pushing open the door without knocking. He was a short man, with a Hitler moustache and fierce round eyes. He squatted opposite me and stared at me like he wanted to attack. His name was Mussie – Moses. He had the intensity of a prophet. I told him I was interested in the fighters. What it had been like to be in the Field.

'Where were you during the war?' he asked. 'We needed help when we were in the Field. Where were you then, when we were fighting? Why didn't you help us then?'

'Many British people did help,' I told him.

'Your government didn't!'

There was a tense silence. 'You can't blame all British people for the actions of the British government,' Awot said. 'Governments and people are not the same.'

Mussie continued staring at me. He thought I was a voyeur of his country's suffering.

'I saw the news reports about the famine and the war was never mentioned,' I told him. 'It is terrible that no one knows anything about this. There shouldn't be a thirty-year war that no one even knows about.'

Mussie sipped his tea. 'Do you know what it is like to try and stop a tank?' he demanded.

'No.'

He sat forward. 'You must come up very close with a bomb and try and blow it up. It is suicide for nine out of ten people who try. But you have to do it; there is no choice. You must sacrifice yourself.'

Awot poured more tea, and then began to speak quietly. 'You know, during the Sixth Offensive people were moving all night. The injured were coming back, and when they were healed – no, before they were healed – they returned to the front. They were not forced to do it – they volunteered. They would hide from the doctors and nurses, and go back to the front at night. If you had no shoes then you went barefoot, if you had no clothes, if you were ill. Men and women with artificial legs can shoot a gun. Men and women without legs are fearless fighters. They know that they can't run away. They never retreat.'

I could feel Mussie's eyes burning into me. 'Yes, sick people would fight,' he said. 'Everyone wanted to go to the front and fight. So many of my friends were sacrificed. But we couldn't have beaten the Ethiopians without the help of the people. They helped us: they carried our ammunition, they carried the wounded, they fed us. We would have been beaten without the people.'

There was a brief movement of air; the trees whispered amongst themselves. I saw Senait shiver. 'When Mengistu launched the Sixth Offensive we listened to his speech on the radio and then we dug our trenches deeper and waited for him,' she said. 'We tuned in to the Ethiopian radio as he was making a speech in Addis football stadium. We listened as he smashed a bottle into pieces. He declared he would smash the Eritreans in the same way.

'It was very terrible. We only stopped the Ethiopians with our bodies. There were once sixty tanks against one hundred and twenty fighters. It was very terrible.'

We drank more tea, and talked long about the war and their lives in the Field. Then it was time I went. I walked back through the streets and noticed how quiet they were. All the compound gates were shut. There was the sound of a radio playing music; a man was singing; some women were clapping.

This was peace.

In the Field, Awot worked in the EPLF education division. Young fighters were educated in political theory and the history of Eritrea in the Revolutionary School. The Eritreans had been fighting for twenty-eight years already, and no one knew how much longer the struggle for liberation would take. Young students were trained to continue the fight, in case the leaders grew too old to continue. The children were taught their history so that they would understand why their parents had taken up the gun, and when their parents were dead they would not let the fight die.

In the Revolutionary School students were taught about equality, democracy, socialism, revolutionary theory and Marxism-Leninism. It was a bizarre situation: Marxist rebels fighting a Marxist government supported by the USSR. They all shared policies of social reform: nationalisation, literacy, equality, the establishment of a 'people's democratic state'. But the Ethiopians were invaders. Their war machine had devastated Eritrea. The Eritreans wanted a free country, Eritrean Marxism not Ethiopian Marxism. Ethiopian Marxism brought oppression, slaughter and famine.

Revolutionary School classrooms were under large boulders or dug into the hillsides, to hide them from the Ethiopian fighter jets. But sometimes the jets would find them.

One day some boys in Awot's class were in the open, playing football. They were spotted by a jet fighter and napalmed before they had time to run for cover. Awot watched the boys writhe on the floor until the burning petroleum jelly had erased the human features from their faces and they were unrecognisable smudges – like half-made bodies of clay.

The fighter planes came back after ten minutes to pick off anybody who had come to help the boys, but all the bodies had been moved already. They only left an unburnt football lying on the ground.

The night after he had buried half his students Awot decided to learn Arabic. His teacher was a female fighter called Selma Sa'adin. As she guided his hand over the flowing script of the Prophet, they fell in love. Awot learnt quickly.

A year later, Selma was assigned to carry messages to an underground cell in Asmara. It was dangerous work, and on her third mission she was captured. The Ethiopian secret police didn't expect to be in Eritrea much longer so they wanted to make sure they were never forgotten. Captured EPLF rebels could not expect to live; all they could hope for was a quick death. But Selma was not killed quickly. She was raped and tortured for two weeks. She died in her cell after a five-hour session with an Eritrean torturer. When Awot heard she had been captured he began to study child psychology. When he was told of the manner of her death he redoubled his efforts.

Awot told me this as we drank more Melotti than was good for us. His voice wasn't emotional, it did not break. He was so calm that I almost forgot that this was actually his life, not just a story you read or hear. Around us Eritrean men sat smoking and talking, and above our heads waiters shouted out drinks orders. It was as if everyone had been here enjoying themselves since the year dot, and there had never been a war. I told Awot that he seemed very calm, and he looked surprised.

'I was lucky,' he told me. 'Many other people lost much more than I did.'

With each death Awot took up a new topic of study, as if the way to defeat death was by learning. Knowledge was something that needed to be cherished and protected, for the time when the killing would stop.

———

When the USSR collapsed under the expectations of *glasnost*, the Soviet government pulled the plug on Mengistu's regime. The tide of war had been moving inexorably in favour of the rebels, and the collapse of the Soviet Union helped speed up its conclusion.

By 1989 the EPLF had the eleventh largest army in Africa. They had begun to take on the Ethiopians in conventional set-piece battles, and win. In January they won the largest tank battle of the war, destroying thirty-seven Ethiopian tanks in the coastal lowlands. In February they captured Massawa. By spring they had taken almost the whole of Eritrea and were helping the other Ethiopian rebels, like the TPLF (Tigray People's Liberation Front), advance on Addis Ababa. The Tigray were the northern tribe of Ethiopia, culturally close to the Eritrean Tigrinya; divided only by the Italian colonisation.

Justin Hill

On 19 May the Ethiopian lines around Decamhare collapsed and the EPLF moved in on Asmara. On 22 May Mengistu boarded a plane and fled to Zimbabwe, to the arms of his friend Robert Mugabe. His Communist dream was sucked down the drain of history with little more than a gurgle.

On 24 May 1991, the 120,000-strong Ethiopian garrison, abandoned by its leaders, was surrounded and cut off by the EPLF in the capital, Asmara. They decided to flee but the roads to Ethiopia had been cut. They fled west to Sudan without food or water. There were 120,000 of them fleeing 60,000 Eritrean fighters. Many died on the way. Their families were not there to bury them. They were young and leaderless and a long way from home. Their bodies rotted on the roadside for weeks. The whole stretch of road stank of dead.

Five minutes after the Ethiopians withdrew, the EPLF tanks rolled into Asmara. The inhabitants were confused – they had just watched the Ethiopian tanks leave when the Eritrean rebels drove in. It took them a few minutes to realise what was happening.

The old men and women tore down fronds of trees and danced ecstatically in the streets.

The fighters danced on their tanks, and waved their guns and their flags of green, yellow and red.

Students danced as they poured out of school.

Children danced without knowing why.

Naked babies danced in their cots.

The party raged for days. The Eritrean people had won a thirty-year war without outside help. They had defeated the enemy: Haile Selassie backed by the US and then Mengistu

Haile Mariam backed by the USSR. They felt that they had beaten the world.

———————

Expats said Asmara was boring. So did the US-Eritrean returnees. They hung around in groups for protection from the moral tone set by those who had never left.

'Why did you come here?' I asked one young boy from the US who was hiding inside an immensely hooded top. His basketball boots were five sizes too big for him; his laces were undone.

'My folks are, like, from here.' He dribbled the sentence out. Then he asked me, 'Why do you . . . like – come here?'

'To work,' I told him.

'What you doing?'

'Teaching,' I said. 'Teaching English. In Keren.'

He whistled. 'Phew!'

I looked back at him.

'But Jeez, man,' he whistled, 'this place sucks!'

He was right, of course: Asmara *was* boring; there was nothing to do but drink Melotti, which was the worst beer on the planet. And Asmara was boring even with the amount of Melotti that was drunk. But he was missing the point: this was peace.

It was a Sunday morning when I managed to find the tank graveyard on the outskirts of Asmara – five acres of hardcore desert buried under a stockpile of US and CCCP trucks and weapons. There were armoured cars, trucks, motor bikes, twisted scraps of metal. Further in were the tanks, rank after

rank of killers: solid, fearsome, expensive, meticulously researched and tested.

There were tanks of all descriptions: new, old, American and Russian tanks; tanks with the dark hole at the end of the barrel still aimed at you; tanks with neat holes in their carapaces from armour-piecing shells; tanks haunted by the ghosts of thousands; tanks with their intestines shattered and fused; tanks without turrets; tanks with cacti growing in their tattered shells; rank after rank of tanks. I stood alone and my skin prickled. The machines still gave off an aura of fear, as if the broken, twisted corpses might suddenly return to life.

I thought of the skill and education and effort that had gone into producing these monsters. All of them were cleverly designed and lovingly created by intelligent people in the USA or in European countries. They were a testament to the amount of money the world powers are prepared to invest in bolstering their strategic interests. A testament to the ingenuity and skill the world invests in war.

———

The night before I left for Keren, Awot came round unexpectedly. He had a present to give me – a list of names of people he thought I should meet.

We started talking about the future, and as we talked I asked Awot what made the Tigrinya, Tigre, Afar, Bilen, Baria, Kunama, Hidareb, Saho and Resaida – the nine tribes of Eritrea – Eritrean? Why had the Eritreans, nine separate linguistic groups and cultures, fought so hard to have Italian colonial borders reimposed, when the rest of Africa was complaining about the problems Europeans had caused in Africa with their artificial borders? It was as if Eritrea was swimming against the tide. Was there more to Eritrean nationality than a response to Ethiopian brutality?

It seemed a question Awot had often been asked, or had asked himself. 'When the British left they wanted to split Eritrea into two. They wanted to put the Muslims with Sudan and the Christians into Ethiopia. But the people resisted. They knew they'd be eaten up in such large countries. So even though they had more in common with Sudan and Ethiopia than with each other, they wanted to stay together.'

'So what is it that makes you Eritreans?' I asked. If a group want to have their own country then they must have a shared identity. What were these shared values in Eritrea?

'The Eritrean experience has been unique,' Awot said. 'We have been colonised throughout our history, and even by another African country. We gained our independence through thirty years of struggle. When no one supported us that had a profound effect on our psyche. Everything we do now, we do ourselves. The experiences of the war are vital to our behaviour now. In a way you could say that the Ethiopians made us Eritreans.'

'You mean by making you decide what you were not?'

'That's right,' he said.

It was ironic that by conquering the country the Italians had given birth to Eritrea, and that the Ethiopians had nurtured it into childhood by trying to destroy it.

'But is not wanting to be Ethiopians enough of a sense of identity upon which to build a country?'

Awot looked at me and smiled. 'No, of course not. It is only a start. Now we must make the people *real* Eritreans.'

I was struck by his use of language. How do you make someone Eritrean, or English, or American? And what happens if the people don't want to be made Eritrean?

'We will do "education",' he told me. 'Like we did in the Field. We will educate the people.' Countries can be fixed by treaties. Nations are impossible to legislate over. Most are born through successive wars.

'Children will be taught civics,' Awot said, 'so that they understand the duties and responsibilities of a citizen. The people will be educated that they have democratic rights. The government will involve the people, and bit by bit they will learn their rights and responsibilities.'

'Won't that take a long time?' I asked him.

'Yes,' he said.

'So how will the government keep the country together until then?'

Awot smiled.

The bus to Keren was a yellow American school bus. The insides had been ripped out, and a replacement interior of plyboard and welded steel piping had been nailed and screwed back in its place. The engine smoked, the music was loud and in the blue morning we eventually pulled out of Asmara bus station and drove out of town, heading north across the highland plateau.

There were six hours of tortuous mountain roads between us and Keren. Winding descents down mountainsides, stomach-churning swings around hairpin bends.

The Italian aristocrat Duke Denti di Pirajno had reported lions here in the 1930s; and I saw a village called Mai Haramaz – Elephant Water – but all the big game was long gone. The war had seen to that: when soldiers weren't killing each other they turned their guns on the wildlife around them. They'd left the land barren: dust and stones, devastated by a virulent plague of human beings.

The only wildlife left were the hunks of burnt-out tanks, melting slowly under the midday sun.

————

Camel car park.

Keren was set at one end of a tear-shaped valley. Around the town the mountains thrust up into the sky, steel-blue in the bright sunlight, hemming in the city like a wall of spears.

'What does "Keren" mean?' I asked a local as I stepped off the bus.

'Mountain,' he said.

Keren lay at the geographical heart of Eritrea. Downhill you were in Tigre Arabia, uphill were the Christian, Tigrinya highlands. The fertile bit in the middle was Bilen.

The town's streets were lined with trees, and in their shade dusty men with white headdresses and sharp pointed chins and beards sat by the road, sipping tea. Their eyes were as hard and dark as the nails on their fingers. Camels loped slowly along the street, pendulum legs swinging under them.

Their lips bobbed in time with their strides, and their lashes fluttered in the bright light.

In Asmara, Aster had told me two things about Keren. The first was that the oranges had the most sweet and exquisite flavour – so much so that in the rest of Eritrea a beautiful girl was called '*aranshi Keren*', 'a Keren orange'. The second was that the road to Keren was like the road to hell; it was paved with sin. What she didn't say was that the particular sin was lust.

The winding road from Asmara down into Keren town was lined with two long rows of houses. They were single-storeyed, whitewashed, and had horizontal wooden shutters covering the windows. The houses hemmed in both sides of the long, hot lane and a half of tarmac, jostling for space. They were the brothels.

A million Ethiopian soldiers died in Eritrea. Dragged from their green lush southern mountains by the hand of a dictator, they came to this hard dry land to fight his war. First they would have been sent to training bases – learnt to kill, been brutalised by tales from older soldiers – and then sent up towards the front. Their last stop was Keren, where they would go and brutalise the whores.

The prospect of death made the Ethiopian conscripts act in many different ways. Some cried, others were impotent, or dreamt of their mothers or sisters or girlfriends, or even the EPLF soldiers waiting for them up in Nakfa. For many of the Ethiopian conscripts a cheap shag with a whore was the last moment of tenderness they had in their life.

The whores lived an isolated life, parallel to society, but they were friendly to people who greeted them first. Infected with HIV, they infected their clients, who infected their families and other prostitutes. It was a deadly circle and a silent killer – never mentioned. In Eritrea no one dies of Aids – they die of euphemisms: a weak heart, tired of life, worms in the stomach.

Even though the soldiers had gone, the women remained because there was nowhere else for them to go. If they had families then these would never take them back, but, with all the killing and famine that had ravished the land, many probably didn't have families to go back to anyway. That was why they had started whoring in the first place. In a country like Eritrea, a girl without a husband or male relative to look after her found that selling her body was the only way she could survive.

———————

I spent the first week living in the Keren Hotel as I looked for a house. I found one in a street behind the brothels and moved in on a Tuesday morning. The house dated from the time of the Italians. You could tell that in the quality of the workmanship. The buildings they were putting up now were concrete boxes with a metal door and metal shutters on the windows. This house was a generation apart. It had a large, dusty yard, which was surrounded by a whitewashed wall, high enough to keep the goats and children out – but not the cats, who lived on the roofs; going from compound to compound along the high-wire walkways of the dividing walls, conducting gang warfare.

My house was of good solid construction, as all the houses in Gezawara'hat were. The name Gezawara'hat meant, literally, 'paper houses', for a reason no one could agree on. Some people said the name came from the fact that the buildings were so poor, which wasn't true. Another said it was because the houses were built by the men in the askari regiments, who sent their letters and money home. And a third theory said it was the area of the old post office, which was also not true. Whatever the reason, my house was not made of paper, but of solid blocks of local stone and a corrugated-iron roof which sloped down in all directions, and walls painted a pale dust colour that would never look dirty. The interior floors were tiled with red and black earthenware, and my windowframes contained glass.

There was Arabic graffiti written in pencil on my walls, from a recently returned refugee family who'd lived there before me. They'd left centimetre marks on the wall to measure their children's height, with each child's name written at their appropriate height: Ahmed, Mohammed, Ismael, Yasmine, 176, 132, 145, 89 centimetres.

The owner of the house was called Ismael: a broad short man with a black bald scalp. He had a squint he hid behind black shades; he cut an impressive figure amongst the other locals in a red bandanna, T-shirt and jeans. I paid him three months in advance in a thick wad of notes that we counted together. There was no need for a receipt.

Ismael's father and uncle had been killed by the soldiers of Haile Selassie in 1972. He told me that all the men of his village were assembled and tied up. Then the soldiers cut their throats. Ismael's mother hid in the fields until the soldiers had left. She found her husband, butchered like a trussed goat, and his brother – still breathing. He was the sole remaining male in his family, and if he survived he would be expected to

marry his brother's widow. With the care of a bride-to-be she
cleaned her brother-in-law's wound, but he was weak from
loss of blood and tormented by a fever. He raved in his delir-
ium about the soldiers with knives, and after three days he
also died. There was nothing left for her, so Ismael's mother
took her children to Sudan the next day.

'And there are people in the Caribbean who worship Haile
Selassie as a god,' Ismael told me as we sat on my steps. 'There
was no rain on the island, and when Haile Selassie came to
visit it started raining! So then they believed he was God!'

Ismael's father and uncle were victims of a deliberate policy
of terror under Haile Selassie against the Muslims in Eritrea.
Throughout the lowlands, where Muslims predominated, soldiers would encircle the villages, round up all the men and kill
them. Sometimes they killed the women and children as well.
When the people all hid in the churches and mosques for
safety, the soldiers found half their work done for them
already, and simply threw grenades through the windows.

'I was too young to remember, but my mother remembers
everything,' Ismael told me after he'd helped me move in and
we shared a cup of sweet tea flavoured with cinnamon. 'They
tied up all the men and cut their throats. This was happening
all over Eritrea.'

'It's terrible,' I said.

'OK, the Italians colonised the country, but they also built
things,' Ismael said. 'The same with the British, they also built
schools for our children. When we were joined with Ethiopia
we had a railway, industry, education and roads. But the
Ethiopians built nothing. They moved *our* industries to
Ethiopia! They pulled up the railway and used the metal to
reinforce their bunkers. They came here and destroyed our

Coffee at Ismael's.

country. Why did they destroy? Why did they just come here and destroy everything?'

As a child Ismael had run away from the refugee camps and joined the EPLF, till the killing got too much for him. Then he left and went to Saudi, where he worked as a driver. In his spare hours he pumped iron in dirty gyms with the other poor migrant workers. He did body-building to drive away the memories of his five years in the Field. In the monotonous movements of dumb-bells and bench-presses he helped to sweat out the memory of war.

'I hated the Arabs,' he said. 'The Syrian Arabs are OK, it's the other Arabs that are bastards. They did nothing to help us. Nothing at all.'

Ismael got rid of the aftertaste of war by growing things. He loved all beautiful things, especially women, and the local

Bilen women more than any others. But he was like the beast to their beauty, and married, so he devoted himself to growing flowers instead. His doorway was veiled by a curtain of bougainvillea. His yard was bright with white jasmine and orchids. He stroked their leaves and petals like they were his children, smelt them, then stood up and smiled.

I planted an English-cottage-garden selection of nasturtiums, daisies and poppies under my window. Ismael came round regularly to watch the flowers grow and bloom. For him they were as exotic as the dark side of the moon.

'You got seeds?' he asked one day when he came to admire. I gave him some seeds, but he wanted more. Ismael could never have enough flowers. He went to Asmara and bought packets of Italian flowers, and sat framing their names in his mouth as he waited for his seedlings to grow. *Tillandsia lindenii, paphiopedilum St Swithin*.

One day I sat with him by the side of the street, watching the Eritrean girls walk past. For him they were more beautiful than flowers, but he didn't stare at the Christian women, because he could see their faces. 'They're too brash,' he spat. 'Like sunflowers.'

Ismael could not take his eyes from the veiled wraps of the Muslim women. Seductive blooms hidden under dense foliage. He evaluated them from the shape of their ankles, as if they were flower stems.

'Do you want to meet Eritrean girls?' he asked me once. 'You want – I introduce.'

'No thanks,' I said.

There was a pause.

'You sure?'

'Yes,' I said. 'Bar girls here aren't my kind of thing.'

'No. Not bar girls. Nice Eritrean woman. Want good time. I introduce you,' he said.

'I'm not that kind of man,' I smiled.

He clapped me across the shoulders with a roar. 'All men are that kind of man!'

There were no streetlights outside the very centre of Keren, so people negotiated their way by memory and moonlight. My way home led me over the dry riverbed and between the brothels. During the day, as I walked into town, the prostitutes sat in loose robes with strings of gold draped across their foreheads. Gold was their only consolation for the nighttime brutality.

They sat and gossiped quietly, occasionally shuffling their bottoms like hens and bursting into loud squawks. Then they would slowly settle down, ruffle their clothes, and settle their bottoms down again. At night they squatted in the brothel doorways and took on a predatory air, vultures ready to pick off the drunks.

The only other regular denizens of the streets were the gangs of itinerant young boys who roamed lawlessly, climbing over walls, stealing fruit, abusing passers-by and running away when people threw stones at them.

One day I came home and found two young men leaning up against the wall of my compound. They stood in the way when I tried to pass so I stopped and looked at them. They didn't seem to be aggressive, they just seemed to have nothing else to do.

I said, '*Selam.*'

They put out their hands, and we shook firmly.

'Speak Tigrinya?' one asked me.

'*K'urub*,' I said. 'A little.'

'Tourist?'

'Teacher,' I said.

'From where?'

'England.'

'England – good?'

'Good,' I said.

'England good – Eritrea good?'

'Both good,' I said.

'England good – USA good?'

'England good.'

'USA good – Africa not good,' he said.

'Africa good,' I said.

'Not good. War – war – war.'

'War – war – war,' he repeated.

'But Eritrea no war,' I told him. 'War finished.'

'Africa not good. Uganda – Tanzania – war.'

'Bosnia?' his friend said.

'No!' he said. 'Burundi – Rwanda – war! Africa not good. Europe good – no war – much money. Much money – no war. Africa – no money – no jobs – no rain – no crops – no food – no good.'

I gave his hand a squeeze and he let go.

'*Ciao*,' I said.

'*Ciao*.'

There were four places that any visitor to Keren had to go to. The first was simple: to sit on the top of the Keren Hotel and watch the sun go down behind the mountains. The second was a visit to the old railway station, which had lost its railway to the war. The tracks had been pulled up and used to

Keren railway, now destroyed.

reinforce Ethiopian bunkers, and the fine old building, Wild West in grandeur, still had dusty platforms where steam trains used to arrive, and the signs on the platform walls still announced in the old Italian spelling – CHEREN.

The next place to visit was the church of Mariam Dearit, the Black Madonna. The church itself was built into a hollowed out baobab tree, and had once been used by Italian troops to hide from British aircraft. At some time some Muslims had tried to burn the church down, and the statue of Mary had been black ever since. Or so the story ran.

The church stood a few miles out of town, along the dried riverbed. Every morning a file of white-robed women would walk out to the shrine to pray, flitting through the dawn like ghosts. In May a great festival would be held, when the Black Madonna would be brought out and paraded by a team of

Procession at the Festival of Mariam Dearit.

drum-beating priests and nuns. It was a wild day of noise and crowds. A morning mass, followed by a procession of drum-beating monks, who danced as they moved, and then an afternoon of goat-stew picnics that left the thinned herds on the dry hillsides in mourning.

But the most famous attraction of Keren was the Senhit Hotel.

The Senhit was the place where all the jobless people went, which made it the epicentre of Keren café life. The building had the expansive manner of the colonial times, and had not been refurbished since. The cappuccino machine would have fetched a high price in the West as a genuine piece of Art Deco design. In fact, the whole interior would.

The Senhit was better known as Arregai's Bar, after the owner: a slender man of medium height, with two-inch-high afro hair that had turned white prematurely. Arregai had been a great footballer in his time, some said the best, and he preserved his taut buttocks in tight grey trousers. Everyone liked to be seen talking to Arregai, but he never stopped longer than to say his 'Hello' and 'How are you?' He worked his clients like a presidential candidate, pumping hands relentlessly. If people had brought their babies to his bar then he would have been photographed kissing them as well.

When Arregai was young, he'd fallen in love with and married a bar girl. They were opposites; he moved relentlessly like a worker bee, while she was rarely seen to move, but sat and munched, like the queen of the café.

Shewita was short and enormously fat. It was impossible to say how much she weighed because she would have broken any scales you tried to weigh her on. What was certain was that she was as wide as she was tall, and her upper arms had a wider circumference than Arregai's thighs. Gold rings had grown into her fat fingers and when she turned her head her jowls swung too, and people standing near by had to duck. Despite her plodding weight, in the structure of Shewita's face and in her wide dark eyes you could still see the beauty of the girl who had captured Arregai's heart.

Arregai's Bar was a place you could come to and where everyone knew who you were. Friends met there daily, not by arrangement, but out of simple habit, and there were even some old men whose seats fitted the contours of their buttocks perfectly. Sometimes, when the waiters moved the seats to sweep the floor, the chairs got put back in the wrong place and you could see the old men fidgeting uncomfortably as they drank.

One of these old regulars was called Berhane, an old man who had iron principles and a chainsaw's sense of justice. He had been an EPLF fighter for twenty years and the experience gave him a crusader's faith in his own ability. Berhane had been burnt by napalm in the Field, and wore a flat cap to cover the cappuccino swirl of white and black skin on his scalp.

When we met in Arregai's we would talk over a coffee or two, and Berhane pronounced edicts on how to solve various conflicts around the world. If he'd been in charge of the UN he would probably have started World War III in about a week.

'Good afternoon, Berhane,' I said once.

He nodded and ordered two more cappuccinos.

We sat in silence.

There was something brewing, apart from the coffee.

'How are things?' I asked.

'Good.' He nodded curtly. 'Thank you.'

The waiter put the cappuccinos down and spilt them both.

'Take your time!' Berhane cursed. 'Look, you've wasted half of it.' The waiter was chained to the floor by Berhane's displeasure. 'Here, clean this – and this!' he ordered, and the waiter did, before slinking off as Berhane tutted, looked around Arregai's Bar and mumbled to himself. I watched him pick up his cappuccino and keep on muttering. The sip restored his humour a little and he turned to face me.

'Why is there war in Northern Ireland?' he said suddenly, pointing a short, blunt finger at me as if I were personally responsible. 'We are a Third World country,' he continued, 'but you are a modern country!' – as though that explained everything. He shook his head.

'Things aren't that simple,' I said. 'It's not about rich or poor, or developed or undeveloped. It's more complicated than that.'

He sat back with his arms folded and bristly. 'So tell me, why are the Irish always fighting?' he demanded.

He wanted a reason, so I gave him one. I summarised a three-hundred-year-old conflict in one sentence: 'Protestant immigrants from Scotland want to stay British, while the Catholic Irish want to join with the rest of Ireland.' He kept his arms folded. 'It's not so different to the war between Eritrean and Ethiopian,' I ventured. 'It's caused by tribalism of the mind.'

'Hmph!' Berhane snorted, then sat forward so he could see the whites of my eyes. 'The Protestants must be sent back to Scotland!' He slammed his fist into his palm.

I nodded. 'But the Scots originally came from Ireland.'

'The Scots came from Ireland to Scotland, and then they went back to Ireland?' he demanded.

'Yes.'

'Are they mad?'

'Many people think so,' I told him.

———————

From a distance the town of Keren looked like a film set for a biblical movie, a little cluster of single-storeyed, flat-roofed houses, bleached white in the sun and huddled together for shade around a fort-topped crag. Asmara was European and Massawa, Eritrea's coastal jewel, was Turkish, but Keren was everything mixed together – African, Arabic and European.

There were minarets and domes, Italian villas facing sleepy roads, and a perimeter of round native *tukuls* with conical straw hats on top. In the centre of town the ground rose steeply, and on top of the rocky crag were the ruins of a fort which was now the Eritrean Defence Force's main base in the area.

Each army that had come to Eritrea had occupied the fort. You could clearly see the defences of the Ethiopians and the Italians, and even the scraps that remained from the Egyptians and Turks. There were the ruins of Haile Selassie's palace, which was destroyed in the fighting of 1977. Many towns-people thought Mengistu had built the fort, as if there was no history before the war for liberation. But the fort and the crag had been here as long as the town of Keren. The fort was probably the whole reason for Keren's existence. In that way, like many towns, Keren was born from the need for protection.

Awot told me he'd looked around the fort when the EPLF had first captured Keren. He'd found a doorway with an inscription in Arabic above a stone plinth that said: ENTER AND SEE WHAT YOU WILL FIND.

'Who carved the inscription?' I asked.

Awot put his head back and said, 'I think it dated back to the time of the Turks.'

'That was a hundred years ago?'

'Yes, more than,' he said.

'Was there anything else there?'

'No, there was only a doorway,' Awot said. 'If there was ever a room then it is now gone. At the time it made me think.'

'Think of what?' I asked him.

'I imagined the doorway was the end of the war. I imagined what we would find when we finally got our liberation.'

'And what did you imagine lay on the other side?'

Awot laughed. 'Everything!'

The local people of Keren were called the Bilen. They traced their ancestry from a people called the Agaw who had raided from Ethiopia hundreds of years ago. The Agaw were renowned as ferocious warriors, and after each raid they returned home with hundreds of slaves and camels loaded with gold. After one of these raids a few warriors stayed and took local wives, and they became the Bilen. The Agaw remained in Ethiopia, their language and that of the Bilen still mutually comprehensible.

The Agaw had a profound effect upon the life of the whole Horn of Africa. All words to do with agriculture in languages like Tigrinya, Tigre, Amharic and Oromo – words like 'plough', 'sow' and 'harvest' – were loan-words from the Agaw language. It was probably the Bilens' use of agriculture that had given them their competitive edge over the other nomadic tribes.

The older people living in Keren remembered the time when the Bilen were feared as warriors. While the Tigrinya had their villages on mountaintops, the Bilen lived in the rich river valleys. In a country like Eritrea you could not live in the valleys without fighting for them, and the Bilen were always happy to fight.

In their oral history the Bilen said that when they came to the Keren valley it was a green jungle of elephants and lions. It was a Garden of Eden, with rich yellow soil and a mellow climate where they could grow things all year round. When their Agaw forefathers came raiding up from Ethiopia and found this vale they set about clearing it of the enemy villagers. Having cleared them away, they must have felt that they were returning to paradise. But over the years they cut down the trees and the rains began to fail.

Fifty years ago the mountains that surrounded Keren were still forested, but during the war the Ethiopians cut them down to stop rebels hiding there, and the people cut down the rest because they needed wood to cook their food. So all the trees were cut down and the soil washed away, leaving rock. Now the valley was stark and naked, as unnatural as a shaved cat.

The Bilen originally settled in villages around the edges of the vale, villages that were now suburbs of Keren town. The names of their settlements had a certain music: Keren Lalai, Shishifeet, Halibmental, Glass. Although they originally came as conquerors, these Bilen villages were now the poor relations of the central town. The war-like Bilen had fallen behind the mercantile Tigre traders, whose cluttered shops jostled for room along the streetside. Now Keren town was mainly Tigre, with a few Tigrinya thrown in.

The Tigre were Muslim herdsmen. Their language and culture were very close to those of the Tigrinya; in fact, not so long ago, they were the same people. The Tigre said that they were all descended from a man called Mohammed Arabi, who came from Arabia and converted their Axumite and Christian ancestors to Islam. The Tigre had many clans and family groupings, each of which followed its individual sheikh, although the Italians and the war had severely disrupted the traditional feudal society.

The Tigre were the men in white jalabias and headdresses who squatted on the roadside, sipping tea. They walked their camels to market daily, delivering wood and water to the narrow streets. The camels spent the day hobbled in the dry riverbed: their deep mourning groans were like the sound of rocks splitting in the heat.

The summer I came to Keren, the rains failed when the crops were half grown. The crops wrinkled to brittle sticks in the ground, and then the rains returned. The grain was past saving, and the people watched their hopes wash away in brown streams of topsoil, a deluge that came like a curse from a wrathful God. The devastating rains continued into September and even October, and the talk in the souq was that this was the beginning of Armageddon. There was a certain irony – a people who could withstand thirty years of human-inflicted warfare had lost the ability to understand a natural disaster.

But on a day when unexpected clouds brought another unseasonable downpour into a blue sunny afternoon I asked a friend, 'Do you think that the end of the world is nigh?'

'No,' he assured me. 'Rain is not mentioned in the Book of Revelation.'

———

After moving my bags into my new house, the first man I went to visit was Abraham, the head of the local education authority. I beat the dust from a linen shirt and paid a shoe-shine boy to give my DMs a shine. The day was hot, oppressively so, so I wore a straw hat and shades a friend had given me in England.

I found the Education Ministry in the old Italian part of town. It was a large square building, a single storey high. There was a veranda running around the outside, and it was decorated with a bas-relief of classical columns. SCUOLA ELEMENTARE was carved above the door, and if you closed your eyes and thought back fifty years you could still hear the voices of privileged Italian infants running around their little colony.

The old school building was made up of four large class-rooms in each corner, and then a few other little rooms and a corridor connecting the whole lot on the inside. Abraham, as chief, had a large room. There was a map of Eritrea behind his desk, and in front a little table and chair for his guests to sit at. The cerulean blue walls were peeling and empty except for a bookcase which had books donated by well-meaning chari-ties – a 1958 cricket annual, jumble-sale rejects and a patched set of early-twentieth-century novels about public-school boys.

'I'm going to be teaching at Meghari School,' I said.

'Ah yes,' he said. 'Welcome.

'If you want anything you should see my vice,' he said, picking some meat out from between his teeth, then: 'I'm leaving next week. I am going to Paris for two years. To study.'

I followed Abraham's directions to his number two. Number two was a fat little man called Faffa, who was almost circular in shape. While a lazy serpent of cigarette smoke curled around Abraham's office, there was a queue of tired teachers trailing away from Faffa's office, continually shuffling and twitching like a rat's tail. Inside his office it was a hotbed of activity.

Faffa didn't get up to welcome me, but half smiled, and rubbed his scalp with the exasperated air of a colonial official who has long ago lost patience with the natives, and then extended his hand for me to shake. It was damp. He wiped his forehead and then the sweat began to break out again.

'Phew! It's like a court in here. I feel like I'm a presiding judge,' Faffa said, and wiped a towel over his head. The sweat reappeared immediately. He spoke on the phone and talked to people in his office simultaneously. Since liberation he had spent half his life issuing the same orders to the same people to do the same things – and the effort of it all made him sweat even more profusely.

'Faffa' was a nickname from the Field. 'Faffa' was the name of food given to children to make them fat. Faffa was certainly fat. He was bald, with round cheeks, and had a stained shirt undone to his navel. Underneath was an equally stained T-shirt. He wouldn't have looked out of place dressed in a nappy with a dummy.

After liberation Faffa had divorced his wife from the Field and married again. The new wife had produced a brood of noisy faces who spilt out of their doorway in an untidy scramble. Their puppy fat gave them an uncanny resemblance to their father.

'Was this the Italian elementary school?' I asked.

'Yes. And now it's the Ministry of Education. It shows what has happened to our country in the last forty years. That's why we need people like you. Thank you for coming.' Faffa stopped, and frowned. 'Have you moved into your house?' he asked me, and I told him that, yes, I had. 'Oh good,' he said, and his mind went off on things he had to tell other people, then he turned back to me. 'You're at Meghari School, aren't you?'

'Yes.'

'Good. It's along the road to Agordat, on the left, you can't miss it. If you need any help, then I'm your man.'

———————

I found Meghari School the next day. There were no students because the students knew the teachers would be late, and there were no teachers because the teachers knew that the students would be late. The store keeper was sitting on a chair under a low tree by the office block, whose shade doubled as the staffroom. He smiled and waved and took about twenty florid sentences to welcome me to Eritrea and Meghari School.

Inside the office I found the headmaster, Igzaw Haile. He was a fighter, and looked like a teenager. At the moment I met him his desk was besieged by thousands of illiterate parents trying to fill out the forms that would enable their children to enrol at the school. A few had planned ahead and brought a child along to do the reading and writing, but others were confusedly attaching their thumbprints to all the wrong places. I fought through the crowds of people and found Igzaw behind his desk.

'When does term start?' I asked.

'It's started!' he grinned.

'Has it?'

'Yes, it started last week.'

'Ah. So where is everyone?' I asked him.

'Asmara,' he replied. 'We are registering students now,' he continued. 'Come back next week.'

I turned to leave and he said, 'Justin.'

'Yes?' I asked.

'You're flying low,' he grinned, 'without a licence!'

One of the reasons teaching in Keren was so hard was the shortage of teachers. When the Eritreans voted for independence the Ethiopian teachers, who made up the majority of the teaching staff, upped and left. To replace them were the educated soldiers of the EPLF and the Eritreans who returned from Ethiopia. But they were not enough.

The war had disrupted education so much that for many children in the villages there was no chance of a schooling, or that schooling was in Amharic, the Ethiopian language; so that now, with freedom, all that backlog of students was coming through. The classes I taught had around seventy-five students each, of all ages between eleven and twenty-five. The numbers problem was so acute, and the number of schools and teachers so small, that the education authorities ran a 'split-shift' system. Each school had two schools' worth of students. The first shift started with assembly, flag-raising and singing the national anthem at 7 a.m. That meant students and teachers had to be at school by 6.45 a.m. Lessons would continue through the morning, with a short break, and finish at 12.30 p.m., when all the morning's students would go home. As they were going home the afternoon shift would arrive, at about 12.45 p.m., for assembly at 1 p.m. Then lessons would continue for the afternoon shift, with a short break, until 6 p.m.

It was at school that I came face to face on a daily basis with the myriad problems that wars leave in their wake. There were the children who'd survived stepping on landmines; they had usually lost one or two legs up to above the knee, and also one or both eyes. There were the children whose parents had been killed and who lived with relatives; aunts and uncles would be responsible for as many children as were left to them. They turned up on parents' day and did a tour of the school, enquiring about each of their charges. But most of the effects were more subtle.

There were disturbed children, who had seen people raped or murdered – often family members like parents, brothers or sisters. There were children who had been born and had grown up in Sudanese refugee camps, and saw little point in education. Students whose families – displaced refugees or simply people unable to get a job in Eritrea's ravaged economy – didn't have enough money to feed them. There were the couple of students who every year died of diabetes, or caught TB or a simple disease like dysentery or giadia. The children with these illnesses stopped coming to school all of a sudden, and then the message came through, weeks later, that they'd died.

These kind of life experiences meant time in the classrooms, where eighty students sat three to a desk and three to a book, was as much about crowd management as teaching. Fights over book space, missing pencils or how much seat each student got were regular. Copying was endemic. Lethargy was also compulsive for some students. There were times I almost broke down because it was all so hopeless. Sometimes I woke up in the middle of the night and couldn't sleep. Those were days I dreaded stepping into the classroom.

Each day started with assembly. Teachers would take a stick and chase students out of classrooms and from behind walls, and herd them into line. The students loved the daily chase and excitement of it all: there was a constant escalation of tactics on both sides as term progressed. The teachers would begin to throw stones at the students, who would whoop and yell; students would leap out of classroom windows and run behind the back of the class; teachers would work in pairs, stalking both sides of the classrooms to catch all the students.

The daily stress of work and its conditions compounded the poverty we all lived in. I got the same wage as my colleagues, which worked out at £60 a month. The low pay contributed to the demoralisation of the teaching staff, all of whom had children or parents to care for. Their euphoria had quickly evaporated after independence when they realised what liberation meant for them.

They blamed the students' poor discipline on a number of things: some said it was the history of revolting against the old rulers; others that the economy was so devastated that there were no jobs for people with an education. Many agreed it was because the way to prosperity in Eritrea didn't lie in education, but in whether you'd been a fighter with the EPLF – or not.

This was certainly a problem. The whole education system was run by EPLF fighters, from the Minister of Education to the director of each school. Some of the fighters deserved their positions; others did not. The ministry preserved the command-style system of management that they had used in the war, but which was unsuitable for civilian staff and civilian life. There was a highly centralised system of control, with no question of discussion; management was a matter of issuing orders. Many of the fighters had ill-disguised contempt for the teachers who were educated under the Ethiopian system, who wore good clothes and were fluent in Amharic, danced to the tunes of Mahmud Ahmed and looked to Addis Ababa, not Asmara, as the cultural centre of their lives.

The conditions in the school ground everyone down fairly quickly, and towards the end of term violence became depressingly common. I was shocked at first to see teachers punching or kicking students, but it soon became an irregular event. Occasionally teachers would have to be dragged off by colleagues and pulled back to the staffroom. There was always the grinding oppression of overwork, stress, extreme physical conditions. By the end of the twenty-week terms we were all utterly exhausted, a deep fatigue that hollows you out to a shell.

Once my friend Habtewolde, one of the teachers in the English Department, found two grade-six students who had kidnapped a grade-seven girl and were raping her in one of the old Ethiopian trenches. He trussed them up and dragged them back to the staffroom. The police were called. They brought their cattle prods with them. When the students saw what was happening, they charged out of their classrooms and gathered to watch.

Violence had become such a part of the national psyche that some people weren't able to let go. In a horrible way I think many of the teachers and students in the school were addicted to it.

It was towards the end of my first term that I found myself so angry with a student that I grabbed him by the shirt and raised my hand to punch him. The class went silent. Someone at the back giggled.

That night I went for a beer at Arregai's and then walked home through the narrow streets of the souq and along the riverbed. The brothels were busy: the lights were on and the music was loud. I got home, put on some music and lay in bed with a candle. I was still tense, could still feel the anger. I imagined punching the student, how I would have felt if I had; then blew out the flame and wondered what the hell this country was doing to me.

The book I taught from was the *English for Eritrea Grade Seven* textbook. It was a book specially designed for Eritrea after liberation, covering a newly designed syllabus, which was taught in English from grade eight and above.

Chapter One was about people, and contained all the vocabulary necessary to describe the people of Eritrea's different tribes: 'headscarf', 'traditional dress', 'plaited hair', 'beard', 'moustache'. Chapter Two covered animals, and had two pictures comparing Eritrea in 1940 (an unlikely collection of lions, hyenas, giraffes, elephants, zebra and something that looked like a fox, all gathered by a water hole in a forest) with Eritrea today: a cracked and broken landscape that looked like the remains from a nuclear holocaust. It introduced the idea of good husbandry and caring for animals, and ended with a piece about camels and how they were used in the war for liberation.

The rest of the book covered subjects such as Smoking, Save Our Trees, Travel and Transport, Women in Eritrea, Jobs, Aids.

Oral test:
Teacher: How do you practise safe sex?
Student: Use a condom!
Teacher: And what should you do before getting married?
Student: Have an Aids test.

Teacher: And?

Student: Make the man have an Aids test too!

Teacher: And how is the HIV virus transmitted?

Student: From mother to baby. From – erm – blood-to-blood contact. And – erm . . .

Teacher: Yes?

Student: Sexual contact!!

Teacher: Very good.

The unit on Women in Eritrea was more controversial. Repression of women, by men and by other women, was so thoroughly integrated into Eritrean life that to try to remove it meant unpicking every seam that made up the tapestry of culture and daily existence.

It would take years, probably much longer than the war against the Ethiopians.

The plight of women in Eritrea was brought home to me by the fate of the first student I expelled from my class. Expulsion became my punishment of last resort, one the students feared more than a beating.

The girl was called Almaz, a pretty seventeen-year-old who never brought books to school, never did any work. She habitually turned up late for lessons; was caught sneaking in and out of school; didn't see the point of pretending to care.

She was warned. Warned again. Her guardian came in for a meeting. She and her guardian signed an undertaking to improve. She didn't.

I went through three rounds of warnings and she signed a series of declarations and apologies before she qualified for an expulsion. I heard that after she was expelled she continued living with her two brothers. It was a few months later that I asked again and no one knew where she was. It was strange that no one knew in such a small place as Keren.

'Where's she gone?' I asked Ismael, who knew the family.

'Oh she's left town,' was all he said.

'And?'

He was more interested in the poppies under my window.

'And?'

'She joined her two brothers. Bad men. Only spend money their mother sends from Saudi!'

'And!'

'I don't know.' Ismael stroked the poppy petals gently and watched them nodding at each other in the breeze. 'You got more seeds for these?'

While we shared a cappuccino at Arregai's I asked the sports teacher, a brusque and direct kind of man, and described the girl I meant.

'Almaz!' the teacher said. 'Yes, I know. Almaz Estifanos. The mother decided to stop sending money to her children because they just wasted it. She cut them off. One of the sons went into the Army, the other landed himself on some friends, and Almaz went to Hagaz to be a prostitute, but she's too thin.' The teacher shook his head with indifference. 'In Eritrea men like big women. Like Arregai's wife.'

He nodded in the direction of Arregai's wife and I appreciated what he meant. She was bigger than Arregai and all their eight children put together.

'Do many bar girls get married?'

'Some – some,' he thought. 'Prostitutes have no problem, if the man loves her.'

'How much do prostitutes get for one night?' I asked.

'One night! Fifty nakfa,' the teacher said, looking shocked that anyone would want to spend so long with a whore, 'but for one intercourse fifteen or ten – ten or fifteen. In Ethiopia it is very cheap. In 1982 I was teaching there and one intercourse was twenty-five cents. Now one birr.'

'That's the same as a bottle of Coke!'

'No, Coke is twenty-five cents cheaper,' he said.

I thought he might have been joking, but he wasn't.

'So fifty nakfa a night is a lot of money.' I said. 'Teachers only get three hundred and fifty nakfa a month – so prostitutes must get quite rich.'

'Yes, but no save. They spend on clothes, make-up, shoes.'

'What happens when they get old?'

'Prostitutes don't get old.'

'What about Aids? Do they use condoms?'

'Prostitutes don't mind. Condoms or not,' he said. 'As you like.'

———

When Awot knew that I was seriously considering writing a book on Eritrea he suggested I met a woman he knew. 'She was a fighter, but now she's the President of the Women's Association,' he told me. 'She'll be able to tell you all about the role of women in Eritrean society.'

Men in Eritrea joke, 'We love our animals more than our women.' Like many jokes it cuts close to the truth.

'Women are cheaper than cows,' Nejat insisted, and the beads in her dreadlocks rattled. 'A woman's dowry is only a few grams of gold. But cows are worth more than that. Women have always belonged to men, like cattle and land.

That's one of the reasons I joined the struggle, to fight the Ethiopians and also to fight the oppression of women.'

We sat and she ordered two cups of *shahi*, Arabic-style tea, small and sweet. We slurped. Awot had warned me that Nejat was hard, and she looked it. She was tall and muscular. She had a beautiful face, with wide brown eyes and a finely carved nose and cheekbones, chiselled from a block of granite. The whites of her eyes flickered dangerously between her dark skin and the black of her pupils. She was Selma's sister, the girl who had taught Awot Arabic, whom he had fallen in love with, and who was later tortured to death.

When Selma left to join the struggle, Nejat went in the opposite direction, to Addis. She started her career as an air hostess for Ethiopian Airlines. While Selma was in the Revolutionary School, learning the EPLF history of Eritrea, how to clean a Kalashnikov and shoot a man, Nejat was taught to dress her hair in a hundred different ways, how to make up her face, and how to pour tea on a plane without spilling it. Nejat would have looked bewitching in an air hostess's uniform, but if she spilt the tea then you wouldn't have dared complain.

Even though they had started off in such different directions, like families tend to do, the two sisters ended up in the same place: the Field.

The women's movement in Eritrea was started by the male leaders of the EPLF. Revolution was not just a war for independence against the Ethiopians, but also against the traditional laws that oppressed women.

'It was the men who taught us to fight for our rights,' Nejat said.

'So in what ways are women discriminated against?' I asked. Nejat answered my questions without hesitation or embarrassment. Her English was not so good, but with a dictionary and sign language we got by.

1. Women only ate the scraps left over by men. If the men had left nothing then the women would go hungry.
2. Women could not inherit land.
3. Women were culturally prohibited from the kinds of jobs that might give them self-sufficiency, such as ploughing and trading.
4. Villages were run by male-only councils of elders.
5. Tradition forbade women from eating nutritious food during pregnancy, especially meat.
6. These traditions meant the women and their babies were not healthy, and so the women had a much greater chance of dying during childbirth.

'How about female circumcision?' I asked a little nervously after a while.

'What's "circumcision"?'

'It's when . . .' I began, and trailed off.

'Can you show me?'

'Not really. It's when . . .' Her hard eyes nailed me to my seat. 'Pass me the dictionary, could you?'

I found the word and showed her the page.

'Ah-ha!' she laughed. 'FGM!'

'Yes,' I smiled. 'How about female genital mutilation?'

'Oh, I had it done when I was seven years old,' Nejat said matter-of-factly. In the next five minutes there were repeated references to the dictionary for very specialised vocabulary, and I put together the essentials of what had happened:

1. Nejat's mother and sisters held her down by her legs and arms while an old woman cut off her clitoris with a razor blade.
2. There was no anaesthetic.
3. They cut off the outer lips of her vagina too.
4. She was screaming.
5. They stitched the wound back up with twine and bound her legs together with rope.
6. She was left like this for about two weeks as she healed. She couldn't untie herself or walk or go to the toilet. When she needed to she had to just let the urine run down her legs.
7. Unfortunately her urinary tract was blocked by the scar tissue so her mother used a sharpened stick to open it up.
8. When she gave birth to her child her vagina had to be cut open.

'FGM is supposed to stop girls becoming sex workers,' Nejat told me. 'One of the problems we have is that in Eritrean society it is women who enforce these customs. When I was circumcised my mother asked me, "Do you think a woman looks better with her mouth open or closed?"' Nejat stopped to laugh. 'She was saying that a vagina with a small hole is better. The women in Eritrea are all very conservative, more so than the men. It is the women who keep these practices going. They say, "It happened to me and never did me any harm, it should happen to you." It is the women who need to be educated most.'

Semhar was too young to be a fighter. She had come of age in the early years of peace, and was conscious of her role in the future of Eritrea, an educated woman in a tempest of prejudice. Semhar was a beautiful girl, a rag-doll with shoulder-length dreadlocks. Her voice was like that of a father's favourite child, and she had a sweet almond face to match.

She told me she was at Asmara University.

'So what would you like to do after graduation?' I asked.

'Journalism, or teaching,' she said vaguely, then with more conviction, 'but I really want to be a preacher for Jesus.'

'Oh. How nice,' I stalled. 'What kind of Christian are you?'

'What do you mean?'

'Catholic or Orthodox?' I said, choosing the two major forms of Christianity in Eritrea.

'I follow the Bible, the Bible is the Word of God, I am a Christian, enough,' she said like she'd just explained three times three equals nine to me, then asked: 'Do you believe in Christ?'

'I believe he existed. But I don't believe he was the son of God.'

'So where do you come from?' She now plunged into a frontal assault.

'My mother and father,' I said.

'No, where do people come from?'

'Apes.'

'And apes?' she persevered.

'Fish,' I said.

She changed tack. 'And where does all creation come from? Who started it all?'

'I don't know,' I said. 'Maybe nothing or never, maybe it has always been and always will be.'

'I know there's a God,' she told me with a smile that could melt men's hearts. 'Look at all the mountains, trees, flowers and people. I know He created them.'

'Maybe,' I said, 'but you can't prove it to me.'

'"He who believes shall have everlasting life,"' Semhar quoted. 'Also, "Those who believe, their households will be saved." So my family will also be saved. I know this will happen. It's happening now.'

'So is there money in being a preacher?'

'Just being a Christian pays. I am always receiving His bounty. And I know,' she tapped her breast, 'that I will have life everlasting.'

'But what about money? You'll need money to survive.'

'God will provide everything.'

'It's our way,' Awot told me afterwards. 'We have always believed in God, and the war made our faith stronger. Or destroyed it completely.'

'Do you believe?' I asked him.

'With my history it is difficult to believe in God,' Awot said. He looked past my face and then down into the bottomless swirl of his cappuccino. 'If there was a God He would never have allowed those things to happen. People who talk about Him punishing us for our sins are talking utter rubbish. How have the Eritrean people sinned so much more than any other country? There is no God.'

I was in Asmara for a weekend and Semhar invited me around to her single-room house for dinner.

'I have a friend coming,' Semhar told me as she stirred a pot. 'I thought you'd like to meet her.'

'Thank you,' I said.

'She lived in Addis until after liberation. It wasn't easy for Eritreans living in Ethiopia during that time.'

'Sounds interesting,' I said. 'How are relations with Ethiopia since Mengistu fled?'

'Very close,' she said. 'The new government of Ethiopia is headed by Meles Zenawi and the men of the TPLF. The TPLF were EPLF allies in the war against Mengistu. They fought together to drive him out. After the referendum the new Ethiopian government let Eritrea break away without a struggle. In fact the two presidents are cousins.'

I nodded and sniffed appreciatively. 'So what are you cooking?'

'First dlot, then zigne,' Semhar said.

'A-ha!' I said, but it left me none the wiser. 'Can you buy it in the shops?'

She scratched her head. 'It is difficult, because it's made up of lots of different things. It's hard to buy them all from the butcher. For dlot you need stomach, intestines, liver, pancreas, and this' – she pointed to part of her stomach – 'what's the name for this?'

'I don't know,' I said, and I wasn't sure I wanted to.

'Oh well,' she continued, 'the easiest thing to do is to go to the market and buy a goat. You take it home and kill it and then you have all the bits you need. With the meat you can make zigne.'

'I see.'

When Semhar's friend came we all sat around a wide plate of injera, a thin sourdough crumpet about half a metre across. It was the plate and spoon for the meal: Semhar upturned a bowlful of dlot into the middle and then poured a ladle of red zigne stew around it. We tore off pieces of the injera and used it to scoop up bits of meat and sauce. Semhar kept ladling out more strips of injera, and more spoonfuls of the spicy zigne, and as we munched on pieces of meat I chatted to her friend, who was called Hidat.

Hidat was an enormous woman, with breasts, stomach and buttocks that were huge and rounded like sacks. She looked like a hippo in a yellow dress. If she was naked and squatting then she would have been a pagan Earth Mother, like the Venus of Vestonice. But despite her size and weight she stepped lightly, as if she repelled gravity – or that gravity was repelled by her.

After the meal sunset brought darkness rushing in like some-one late for work. Hidat lit a hurricane lamp, and we sat back on the two beds that we'd been using as chairs. The weight of the meal and the flame's dance gave the darkness a dreamy silence. Semhar squatted to wash the bowls and then made tea. Hidat shifted her weight from left buttock to right buttock and back again. The steel-framed bed groaned in protest. I could feel her eyes watching me, and in the silence a question was brewing up like a thunderstorm on a hot afternoon.

'Why don't you speak?' Hidat asked me suddenly, as she licked her fingers of the stew. The dance of the flame seemed to stop, and I looked in my mind for something to say. There was a postcard behind her head of a 747 in Eritrean Airlines livery. I was certain that Eritrean Airlines was a one-office affair on Liberation Avenue, an outfit that did not extend to a 747.

'I didn't know Eritrean Airlines had any big planes,' I started. 'I thought they only had a light aircraft that runs from Asmara to Assab twice a week.'

Hidat nodded. 'This plane was donated by the Norwegians for two years. But it was too expensive to run. Now it has been returned.'

'Really? Did it use to do international services?'

'I don't know,' Hidat said quickly, and silence settled over the room with the evenness of dust that had been disturbed. We sat and looked at each other. I thought of something else to say. I thought of the food and the fact that Semhar's family bought a live goat every week from the market.

'Do most people eat meat every day?' I asked.

'Why do you ask so many questions?' Hidat countered.

'Because your life here in Eritrea is so different from life in England.'

'Is it?' she asked, amazed.

Her answer amazed me in turn. 'Yes, of course it is,' I said. 'Very different.'

She shook her head in wonder. We grinned at each other across the chasm of cultures.

'So where do you live?' Hidat asked.

'York, England,' I said.

'New York?' she asked.

'No. Old York.'

'What is it like?'

'Bigger than Keren, smaller than Asmara.'

'You ask us so many questions,' Hidat said. 'I want to know what it's like where *you* live.'

Semhar came to sit next to me. 'Yes, I want to know what your life is like,' she said.

'I don't know where to begin,' I told them.

'Just try,' Semhar soothed.

I told them about the village I grew up in on the edges of the

city of York. I told them how each summer the streets would be
packed with tourists, with ubiquitous crowds of foreign school-
children who swarmed in denim gangs with matching neon
backpacks slung over one shoulder. Each winter Japanese tour
parties smiled and nodded their cameras at everyone they saw,
and then took photos of themselves standing rigid and unsmil-
ing in front of anything that stayed still long enough. I said it
felt like I was living in a museum sometimes. I've been caught
in the background of so many people's holiday snaps, walked
through so many home videos, I feel like an anonymous film
star. People in Japan and the US have seen me a thousand times
without knowing who I am. I laughed and stopped.

Hidat and Semhar were mesmerised.

They encouraged me to go on. I told them about the industry in York, and said that apart from the Post Office and the
railways there were only three factories. The sugar-beet factory was next to the river, and gave off a smell of peanut
butter. Terry's chocolate factory was the other side of town,
while not far away, completing the triangle, was Rowntree's.
Each morning when I woke up I could tell in which direction
the wind was blowing because of the smells in the air – peanut
butter was a south-westerly, the smell of Smarties and Yorkie
bars was always an easterly sea breeze, while the north wind
was Black Magic.

When we were very small my family spent summer holi-
days in a farmhouse on the Cornish coast. We would have
two weeks of Cornish pasties, seaside towns and tin-mine
museums and then we would pack up the car and drive back
up to York. Cornwall seemed like the end of the world then.
Our preparations for the drive home would last for days,
making sandwiches and Thermos flasks of tea. Buying books

and games for us to play on the way. Being loaded on to the back seat at night as we began our fourteen-hour journey at 11 p.m. to avoid the traffic. I'd lie awake and watch the harvest moon set in the car window.

I stopped again and realised that they were listening to me as if I were telling them a fairy tale.

When I'd finished there was a long silence. Hidat was the first to speak. 'I have a friend who has many relatives abroad, some in Sweden, England, the States and the Emirates. They tell me I am better off here, where I can get an education. If I was in England I would have to work.'

'Yes, I think it is better if you stay here,' I told her, and it was true. She was Eritrean, and Eritreans should live in Eritrea. Once they left they would stop being Eritrean, and Eritrea needed educated people for the years ahead, especially young, educated women. Semhar poured tea, which tinkled as the liquid dripped into the small cups. She was wrapped in thoughtful silence as she dug out spoonfuls of sugar and stirred them into the tea. Hidat and I still looked curiously at each other.

'Semhar said you used to live in Addis,' I began. 'What was it like living there during the war?'

'We used to pretend we were Amharic,' she said, 'except my mother. She didn't learn Amharic because she didn't want to be called up to perform traditional Tigrinya dancing. You see, if she'd learnt Amharic then she'd always have to do Tigrinya dancing for foreign dignitaries to show how happy we were under Ethiopian rule. My mother couldn't do that.'

'Are there many Eritreans still in Addis?'

'Oh yes, many,' Hidat said. 'Many came back to Eritrea after liberation but they went back again because there are no jobs here. In Eritrea the wages are low and everything is expensive. It is all right being free, but if you cannot work then it is a fool's paradise.'

The last person I met at the end of my first year in Eritrea was a young girl who came up to talk to me at a wedding. She was dressed in jeans and a T-shirt, an Eritrean who had grown up in Germany, where her family had fled when she was a baby. When she was sixteen she watched the German TV news showing the EPLF tanks riding back into Asmara, and the Ethiopians fleeing. She couldn't remember Eritrea, but her mother couldn't forget.

At night she dreamt of the country, her family and the life she had left behind. After liberation her mother began to prepare to return to Eritrea, and decided to take her daughter back with her. Plucked from Germany at sixteen years old, she had been dropped in a traditional African society that was as alien to her as the moon. She told me that she was desperate to go back, away from Eritrea. Anywhere.

'I can talk to you because you are English,' the girl told me, sitting me down in the room as if what we were doing was illegal. She spoke English with a German accent. She'd brought her photo album with her, and narrated each picture to me. 'A friend from school. My swimming club. There's my brother: he's now at Cologne University.'

The pictures showed almost the same life as my own teenage years, except all the captions were in German. At the end all her friends had signed the photo album and written messages of goodbye and good luck. They were all still in Germany but she was here. In this God-forsaken country.

'People criticise me all the time,' she said, working out all her frustrations. 'I smoke a cigarette or go into town in the

evening and they say, "Oh no! Oh no!" I have to go out of
Keren to smoke. When I play sport the people say, "Oh no!
What are you doing? Girls shouldn't play sport!" At school all
my classmates say, "Fuck you, fuck you, go home, fuck you,
you German, go home to Germany." I hate Africa. I hate
Keren. Not good people. "Fuck you, go home!" they say.
"Go back to Germany!" In Germany the people are good. If
there are problems then we talk. I have friends in Germany. I
hate Africa and Keren. The neighbours look at my clothes and
say, "You are wearing shorts. No – not good. Girls can't wear
shorts!" "You are going to town in the evenings. Not good.
You can't do that!" In Germany I watched films, I go out
with my friends, no problem; here, "WAAA! Can't do that,
not good, fuck you, go home!"'

IV

I went to Asmara after the end of term to see Awot. We sat in the American Bar, drank cappuccino and ate blue ice-cream. He remained as committed to the cause and the country as ever. He made me feel ashamed for worrying about my finances. What did it matter if I didn't have enough money, when so many people had died for their freedom? My worries seemed trivial then. I told him this and we both laughed.

'Come on! How about we go on a trip?' he said. 'I have to go to Massawa for some business. Why not come along!'

The next day we woke to a cool clear blue sky and drove out of Asmara, past the Italian and Commonwealth gravesites where men killed in the Second World War were buried.

The Allied troops all had the dignity of a tombstone with their name inscribed on it; the Muslims were buried with their heads towards Mecca. On the other side of the road were long lines of the Italian dead. The white troops had their names and dates; the local troops had ASKARI written on their tombs. Long lines of dead Askari.

As soon as we passed the gravesites the road dropped out of sight and we plunged down. The horizon was full of peaks that were grey silhouettes in the morning mist. A thousand crowded peaks and valleys, jostling away to the horizon. The road descended snake-like across the face of the escarpment in its eagerness to escape, and we spent three hours chasing it.

'Look,' Awot pointed as we went down and down. 'Railway tunnels.'

There were definitely tunnels, solemn stone arches with gaping mouths of black. But there was no railway.

'The Ethiopians destroyed it, didn't they?' I asked.

'Yeah, they pulled it up during the war. They used the rails to reinforce their bunkers.'

The empty gravel track that had once been the railway shadowed the road, the two of them overlapping and coiling around each other like strands in a rope, as we wound down through the spectacular landscape.

'I thought the government was going to rebuild it.'

'Yes, they were. It was the symbol of liberated Eritrea. All the old men who'd worked on the railway in the nineteen-thirties were gathered together and they taught the young people how to rebuild the track. Self-reliance and determination!' He smiled. 'But now the government doesn't talk about it much. The tunnels are too small for the modern lorry containers. It's not really economically viable.'

'It would be a great tourist attraction,' I said, and Awot nodded.

If the Asmara–Massawa railway was ever rebuilt then it would have to be one of the world's most magnificent rail journeys.

As we chased the road down the escarpment I looked out for another Italian project: a seventy-kilometre cable-car-way from three thousand metres up the escarpment to the sea at Massawa, which used to take the fruit and vegetables from the highlands down to the coast, and on to ships bound for Italy.

'From Asmara to Massawa direct!' Awot said.

'Did it take people?' I asked, imagining the cable-car ride. It would make the train journey seem dull.

Awot could see my face. 'No, it was only for vegetables,' he laughed. 'There were five thousand punnets. People used to climb up the supports and steal the food. We learnt that trick from – guess who – the baboons!'

'What happened to the cable-car?' I asked.

'Of course,' he shook his head, 'the Ethiopians pulled it down. It's the story of our country! When the Ethiopians came we had roads, railway and industry, and now – nothing. That is what war produces – nothing. But we are still alive: we can build, we can work to make our country developed again!'

I wasn't sure that Awot was right in saying that war produces nothing. War forces technological advantages, powers social change, and turns peoples into nations.

As we'd descended the temperature and humidity had risen considerably. Now we were nearing the bottom, and we shut the windows and turned the air conditioner on full. The car interior was cool, but the glass of the window was too hot to touch. We free-wheeled down the last bit of the 2500-metre decline, and then the road straightened out, charging off across the shimmering desert.

Awot put his foot to the floor and we chased into the horizon.

'South of here is the Danakil depression' – Awot pointed right, across the undulating scrubland – 'one hundred and twenty metres below sea level. The hottest place on earth.'

'Maybe we'll give it a miss,' I suggested.

We passed the sand-soaked ruins of an Italian fort.

'This is where the Italians were defeated by an Abyssinian leader called Ras Alula.'

'When was he alive?'

'At the time when the Egyptians were pulling out of Eritrea. He was from Tigray, just the other side of the Eritrean border.'

I knew about Ras Alula. He was championed by Ethiopians as a great nationalist. Haile Selassie based his claim to Eritrea on the fact that Ras Alula had conquered parts of Eritrea before the Italians. In truth he was a feudal lord fighting to bring parts of Eritrea under the rule of the Ethiopian emperor. He murdered the local Tigrinya prince. Helped stop the Italian invasion southwards. Died, as so many patriots do, in disgrace.

'He said we were indivisibly part of the same country,' Awot declared. 'And the world believed him. For us he was a traitor.'

At one point there was a train, chugging slowly along its repaired track.

'Where's it going to?'

'Watch!' Awot said.

The train stopped, and then started to go back the way it had come.

'That's not very productive.'

'We've only rebuilt the first forty kilometres,' Awot laughed. 'Patience!'

The land we passed through was so desolate, it was a vision of hell: a horizon of dust and a foreground of desert burning under a livid white sky. Whirlwinds of dust pirouetted like maddened dancers. I spotted a line of cloth-and-woven-reed tents tucked into a gully.

'People live here!' I exclaimed.

'Of course,' Awot said. He liked my astonishment. 'You're just used to England.'

People had lived here in this land, however hard it looked, for millennia. My ancestors must have come here, and then gone north.

'So who lives here now?' I asked.

Awot answered, 'They're called the Resaida. Arabs who came across from Saudi in the last few hundred years.'

The Resaida were the third-newest immigrants to Eritrea, before the Ethiopians and Italians. They were a nomadic people who cared nothing for their surroundings, except that it should offer nourishment to their camels and goats. Their culture matched the environment they lived in: they were a hard, unforgiving people, with rare but spectacular moments of kindness, as overwhelming as an oasis in the sand. But all in all they were better left alone. They certainly thought so, and expressed no interest in anything outside their world. They were only interested in continuing their way of life without interference from Ethiopian or Eritrean governments.

They lived in makeshift camps of reed-mat tents which kept off the sun and which could be moved and rebuilt with the minimum of effort. They had camels and goats but no cows – it was too cruel a landscape for cattle. The men wore dirty white jalabias, and had hawk noses and hard pebble eyes that reflected back the sun's glare. They didn't wave or acknowledge our passing, but wrapped their headscarves around their faces and kept walking into the distance.

'What happened in Eritrea after liberation?' I asked Awot.

'Wa!' he laughed. 'We were too happy! We were finally free. There was no more war, no more killing.'

He smiled as he talked, and I smiled too, because I could imagine just a little of what it was like to be free from war, and free from the threat of death.

'We were so excited because after so much destruction we could start to rebuild our country. We expected the educated Eritreans from abroad to come and help. In America and Europe and the Middle East there were doctors and professors and all the kinds of educated people we needed to help us reconstruct Eritrea. But they did not come. They refused to come back.'

He stopped, and we drove for a time in the silence of our own thoughts.

'Some of them were supporters of the ELF,' he admitted. 'They had their ideas for how Eritrea should be and we had ours. We disagreed and they refused to help. When others came back they asked, "What can you give us?" They wanted us to give them a house and a car, and servants and education for their children.' He shook his head in bewilderment because he, like all the fighters, had been working for free. 'If I phoned up a professor from America and asked him to come back to Eritrea then he wanted to be paid the same money as he was getting in the US. He wanted all things, and we had nothing.

We had risked our lives, given up our friends, and were still working for free. It was very hard for us to understand.

'For me that was a very difficult time!' He laughed with embarrassment. 'I was getting used to civilian life again. In the Field we thought that when we had liberation then we would have so much oil and gas and gold that we could all sit back and enjoy. But since liberation life has become more difficult. We have had to work harder.'

'Harder than in the Field?'

He nodded. 'But what was worse was that we saw other fighters with big mansions – fighters who had watched their friends die were becoming corrupt, and it was very difficult. They were open about it too. They thought no one could catch them.'

'How could they become corrupt after fighting for so long?' I asked, as if Awot would know the answer.

He shrugged, but he was quite happy to talk. 'It is a mystery to me, after everything we went through together in the Field. But then the government started becoming more powerful. They were waiting to see how things would go after liberation. The President warned the fighters that he would build prisons big enough to imprison all of them if they continued to steal money from the people. Now the government is very strict. They will not tolerate this kind of behaviour.'

I nodded. 'So when will Eritrea move towards a multi-party democracy?'

'Our constitution says that any political party must be free of ethnic or religious bias. In Eritrea there are three main types of religion and nine nationalities. This is not a good recipe for many political parties. You know Eritrea is a very small country, with only four million people.'

'That's only a city in America,' I said.

He laughed. 'In Ethiopia they have many parties, meaning-less parties. They have seventy-two tribes and seventy-two parties. That is not politics, that's tribal warfare.'

Awot steered the jeep around the potholes and then said, 'President Isaias says that now we have only room for one party. But in time I think that there will be opposition parties.'

I looked out into the empty blueness of the desert. 'Where will the opposition parties come from?'

'Not from here,' Awot said. 'Not from inside Eritrea.'

We drove on in silence.

Awot suddenly laughed. 'You know, we are not an advanced country. We are still beginning.' He veered around another pothole. 'We have seen the mistakes of other coun-tries. We are still working out which system will suit Eritrea best.' He turned to look at me, and the glare of the desert sil-houetted his face. 'When we wrote our constitution we looked at other African countries, and the problems that they've had. There will be no life-presidents in Eritrea because the consti-tution says the president cannot be president for more than two terms. That has happened all over Africa, but it won't happen in Eritrea!'

I nodded as I took it all in.

'So Isaias Aferwerki is now President,' I said, to get it straight.

'No, because he has not been elected yet,' Awot said.

'So he isn't yet President. But when he is then he will still have two more terms.'

'Yes,' Awot nodded. 'Two terms of four years.'

'And when will the elections happen?'

Awot laughed. He could see what I was getting at.

'And has the constitution come into effect yet?' I asked.

He shook his head.

'So when will it come into effect?'

Awot was still smiling.

'So,' I reasoned, 'all the provisions of free speech, etcetera, aren't valid. Isaias hasn't been elected yet and when he does he still will have two more terms.' He was grinning. I continued. 'Then Isaias could remain not being President until he decides to call elections, and you could have the same problem as other African countries because Isaias might not feel he can give up power.'

Awot laughed again, as if what I was saying could never happen in the Eritrea of his dreams, and as we drove the sound echoed through the desert.

———

The city of Massawa is built on a pair of islands in the Red Sea. Its exact origins are hidden in prehistory, a dark time that fills up the gap between geology and history, between Pliocene and written records. People have probably lived here since before humans were quite human. The city's story is as long as history itself. It was a port even before the rise of the smooth-shaved Egyptians, or profoundly bearded Mesopotamians.

In this time, on the verge of literacy, an unknown people found a way through the mangrove forests, or across the salt blue waves, and decided to settle on the two islands in the bay. This unknown people built their city on one island, and buried their dead on the other. These first settlers would have been amongst the sea-going cultures that flowered in that period, like the Phoenicians and Mycenaeans. Bronze Age kingdoms established on trade winds, by men who sailed in boats with curved prows and painted eyes.

The city's geographical position placed it at a crossroads of the Mediterranean, the long coasts of Africa and India and even further afield. Over time it became a melting-pot of cultures, with traders bringing their own gods with them – pantheons of deities around gods like Zeus, Mithras, Krishna – and the single-minded Jews with their one god, Yahweh. In the first centuries AD Massawa was the second port of the Axumite Empire, second only to the larger port of Adulis to the north, which later silted up and contributed to the Axumite collapse.

But Massawa really came into its own as part of the Arabic world.

When the whole east coast of Africa was the domain of sheikhs and emirs, Massawa was called the Pearl of the Red Sea. Its quays were lined with dhows, and the muezzin's call could be heard by fishermen far out on the waves. In its heyday it was a land of the Thousand and One Nights: to walk through its souq was to walk through a verse of poetry. In this time, before the Italians, it was part of the dynamic community of merchants who traded with the Gulf Arabs, the Mediterranean and Black Sea, India and East Africa. The dominance of these Muslim traders cut the Christian highlands of Ethiopia and Eritrea off from any contact with the Christian world for centuries, during which Massawa stood proudly looking out into the waves of the Red Sea, with Africa at its back.

Now times had changed. Its buildings were in ruins. Its unique combination of inhabitants had fled. Highland refugees

Coral rag compound: Massawa.

filled the ruins. For the first time in more than a millennium, Massawa was now enslaved to an inland government.

Massawa is rumoured to be the hottest inhabited place on earth, though the title is fiercely contested by the inhabitants of a number of places around the world. You'd think their energies would be better spent in going somewhere cooler, but maybe they've managed to get used to the heat. I couldn't, and when the reading on the digital display above the open-air cinema that we passed read 49°C and 89 per cent humidity, I almost fainted from the thought of going outside.

The Italians made Massawa the first capital of Eritrea, while Asmara was being built. Later on, under the Fascists, it became the largest port on the East African coast. The Italians used it as a conduit for all their military hardware shipped in for the invasion of Abyssinia. Now, as we drove through the shoreside suburbs on the mainland, the buildings around us were a pale reflection of their past. Houses and mosques were shells. The road was lined with ruins, with each crumpled wall heavily pock-marked as if a virulent virus had ravaged the very fabric of the town.

Despite the devastation there was hope, of a sort. On the edge of town a newly painted sign stood out from the ruined masonry. The sign was black and white, with livid red letters which read: COCA-COLA WELCOMES YOU TO MASSAWA.

'You see that house?' Awot pointed. There was half a house, with the upper storey torn away by gunfire. 'There used to be an enclosure there where Mengistu dumped the bodies of eight hundred Ethiopian officers who tried to overthrow him.'

I looked at it, and looked away. The tales of the war were sometimes too much. In any other country you visit temples, cathedrals or galleries, but here the only sites of any interest seemed to be those of massacres.

We reached the beginning of the causeway that connects the mainland to the islands. I could see the island with its whitewashed houses around a bay of white sand and mangrove forests, the buildings bright against the hot blue waves of the Red Sea. But instead of heading over the causeway Awot turned left and drove me along a road that led to the salt flats.

'Salt is one of our major exports,' he said as we passed pools of evaporating seawater.

'It'll never make you rich.'

'Money's not everything,' Awot countered.

'That's what I always tell my friends,' I said.

The sun burnt down upon the saline ponds, where lumps of salt crystal mimicked white ice, though it was still 49°C and 89 per cent humidity. It was a vision of Dante's ninth circle of hell. The car crawled along the road and I looked and wondered why Awot had brought me to this particular spot. Then he began to speak, and I understood.

'In December 1977 the EPLF attacked Massawa for the first time,' he said, without turning to look at me. He pulled the car over to the side of the road, and we looked across three hundred metres of shallow sea to the buildings of the old town, on the island.

'I had friends who were there. They captured the land side of the town and bottled the Ethiopians up on the island for months.' He wasn't smiling. 'After a heavy barrage they went into the water to approach the island. They had to wade. It was chest-deep. They went slowly with their guns held above their heads and their feet feeling the way. This was the time that the Russians were helping the Ethiopians. When the EPLF fighters were in the middle of the water the Russian and Ethiopian troops hit them with everything they had: tanks, F5 aircraft, rocket launchers, machine guns and artillery. Even the Soviet warships off-shore. It was too much. They had to retreat.'

I looked across the glare of the water, the blinding sparkle of sunlight on ripples. All was quiet, except for the haunting whisper of the car's air conditioner. I put my hand in to feel the water; it was viscous and body temperature. So that's why it was called the Red Sea: it was like you were swimming in blood.

'The EPLF came back thirteen years later, in 1990.' Awot turned to me and smiled. 'And we used speedboats that time.'

Awot restarted the engine and we drove across the causeway towards the island. At the end of the causeway was a monument, a grey marble base with three rusting tanks upon it. Awot pulled over and we stepped out of the car. We stood under the three tanks and suffered the intense heat. Awot was fired up with zeal. It was a drug. His eyes were wide and he spoke fervently.

'Before the speedboats attacked, these tanks were a diversionary attack along the causeway. The crewmen knew they would die. All the firepower of the Ethiopians was lined up against them. They still obeyed. We had the Nakfa Spirit then.'

I looked at him and nodded, but he was looking up at the tanks. 'Come on,' he said after a long pause, 'let's go.'

We climbed back into the car, and shivered in the sudden chill of air-con on sweaty skin.

'It took us forty-eight hours of fighting to capture Massawa,' Awot told me. 'In revenge, Mengistu ordered the Air Force to bomb Massawa for ten solid days, non-stop.'

———————

Awot had some official business to see to, so I had an afternoon and evening free.

'There's a British man who works at the Ministry of Marine Resources,' Awot told me. 'Why not go and see him? I think he's become quite a local historian.'

I found the Ministry of Marine Resources and asked for Cameron Fraser.

Massawa monument.

'No, sorry,' the man behind the desk said.

'This is the Ministry of Marine Resources, isn't it?'

'Yes.'

'And doesn't a man called Cameron Fraser work here?'

'Yes.'

'Can I see him?'

'No, sorry,' the clerk repeated politely.

I found someone else with an ounce more sense in his head.

'Yes, Cameron Fraser, of course. He'll be very happy for the company.'

'So can I see him?'

'No, sorry.'

As my body melted into pools of sweat I forced out the syllables, 'Why not?'

'He doesn't work here. This is the administration office. Cameron works in the Research Department.'

'A-ha!' I seized on this lead. 'And where's that?'

'I'm not sure, to be honest. I don't have anything to do with that side of operations.'

'What do you mean?'

'It's moved recently.'

'Do you know anyone here who knows where the Research Department is?'

He directed me back to the first man I had talked to. I had just lost five pounds in five minutes in the most extreme form of crash diet. It was too humid to deal with idiots. I approached his desk with an air of resigned exhaustion and sat down to drip puddles on to his chair and floor.

'I'm looking for the Research Department,' I began, expecting that this would take a long time. There was sweat dripping off the end of my nose – drip, drip, drip – on to his desk. I tried to wipe the drips away, but my arm was dripping even more, so I ended up leaving a wet smear across the top.

'That's where Cameron Fraser works,' he said brightly, with only a hint of discomfort from the heat.

'Oh really?'

'Yes!' he beamed.

'So . . .' I wanted to take this slowly, 'where is it?'

'I'll give you a map.'

He did, and at the end of the trail, where X marked the spot, I came across a little man with knobbly knees peeking out from under his shorts. He was white – or, to be honest, pink.

'Cameron Fraser, I presume.'

'Hello, nice to meet you. Come inside – it's air-conditioned. Do you want a drink?' he replied without stopping for an answer, and I thought, This is going to be much, much easier.

Cameron was a botanist funded by the British Overseas Development Agency. He had a plummy accent but had in fact been born and grown up in Egypt; he had never actually lived in Britain. He had spent his adult years in deserted places teeming with wildlife and knew more about the flora and fauna of Ethiopia than the Creator Himself. He had the body of a public-school boy but the face and beard of a Victorian scientist. It was a mammoth beard, wild and woolly, with two eye-holes and a slot for his nose. It reached down to his chest and was an eco-system to itself. His small brown eyes were beads of movement beneath a wide forehead that was creased with education. His eyes darted around like mice and when he talked his fingers would caress his long, mossy beard. He was a man so eccentric that he was almost as endangered as the animals he studied, so I took a photo of him as he washed two cups for us to have a drink.

In Massawa, Cameron was studying the marine environment. It was one of the few places left where the dugong, the sea cow, still existed. War had spent the last thirty years killing people, but it had protected the dugong from humanity.

'But,' Cameron said with factual calm, 'with peace that will change. I'm researching what's here before it all goes.'

He lived in a caravan at the Ministry of Marine Resources Research Station – a stagnant lagoon of green weed and creeping crabs that multiplied like bacteria. His wife and children were back in Britain, where they lived in the Scottish Highlands, in a crofter's cottage a hundred miles from the nearest shop. They never met other people, except for the occasional hiker, and I imagined them in their little family life, washing back and forwards through their daily routines, like seaweed under the waves, unseen and unnoticed. We sat down inside and I glugged down a jug of cool water, then he offered me a cold Melotti. On the table were the sea-smooth bones of some animal.

'A dugong?' I asked.

'Unfortunately not. The locals keep turning these bones over to me. The last dugong was spotted about three months ago by some fishermen, who promise me that they didn't kill it. But these bones don't belong to a dugong, they're from a goat.'

'Good news for the dugong,' I said.

'But not for the goat,' Cameron said without a flicker of humour. He took a swig of Melotti and winced. 'Apologies. Awful beer, but there's nothing else.'

'I know,' I said and grimaced. The first mouthful was always the worst.

When Cameron Fraser wasn't recording the extinction of rare species, he traced the history of Massawa for a hobby.

'It's a long story of a struggle between the sea people and the shore people,' he began, with the air of a man who had a lot to say and was used to being listened to. It was interesting so I sat back and took it all in. 'The first people here settled on the islands because it protected them from the shore people. The Tigrinya name for Massawa is Mitsua – it means "to call". You see, the Tigrinya standing on the shore had to call across to the island for a boat. They didn't have boats, and probably never built them. The Tigrinya are a land people. They still have a mental block about getting on to a boat. It's just not in their culture. A nice example I think is an

Abyssinian king who tried to capture Massawa in the Middle Ages, but he had no boats!'

'Yes, the EPLF tried to do the same thing in 1977,' I said.

'Land people have really never understood the sea. Imagine – trying to capture an island without boats! Quite comic really.'

I thought of trying to capture an island without boats and how it would be funny, except that Awot had just described to me what had happened.

'During the war the whole marine environment within Eritrean waters was left virtually untouched!' Cameron continued. 'In 1991 it was a pristine environment, quite unique in the world. And after liberation the government began by saying all the right things about the environment.' Cameron took a swig and pulled a horsy kind of face. 'But then last month we got a new minister, and he doesn't know a dolphin from a crab. He's only interested in exports. And where does that hard currency go? Buying weapons!' Cameron shook his head, and I responded in kind.

'You know, a few years ago, the government tried to promote fish to the highlanders. This is fish we are talking about: a cheap, healthy source of protein in a country that can't feed itself. But the highlanders had never even seen fish before. They wouldn't eat it. They only want to eat goat. At last the government started giving it out free, but the people just cooked them whole, they didn't even gut them!'

'What happened?'

'There was mass food poisoning!' Cameron exclaimed in wonder. 'So now the government have gone back to the beginning. They've started teaching the people how to prepare and cook fish. They tried to get the people to eat seafood, like lobster. But the people just throw lobster away. The same with tuna and shark. The fishermen think they're worthless and just throw them back.'

'I did notice a lot of oysters on the seafront,' I told him, and he ran aground on my interruption.

'I know,' he said, with a sparkle in his little brown eyes as he tried to remember what he was saying, 'I know.'

He got up and went to fetch another two Melottis out of the fridge. The silence was full of the sound of air conditioner.

'So who do you think were the first people in Massawa?' I asked him when he'd sat down again.

'A good question.' He recovered his train of thought. 'A mix, really: merchants from Egypt, Greece, Rome and the Persian Empire. India as well, and the Chinese probably came here at some time. I like to think of Massawa as a kind of free-trade centre for ships of the ancient world.'

'A Singapore of the Red Sea?'

Cameron Fraser gave me an eagle stare, long and impenetrable. 'Umm,' he said.

'And what did Massawa trade in?' I asked.

'Oh, the usual stuff. Purple dye, incense, coffee, ivory, slaves. Pretty much standard, really. But in my opinion the original reason for people to come here was salt.'

'Oh really?'

'Yes! The one sure way of making money.'

I raised my eyebrows.

'You see, along this whole coast there aren't many places suitable for drying salt. But here there are – salt flats.'

I sipped my beer. 'And how does salt make you rich?'

'Salt was vital for the people who lived in what is now Eritrea, Ethiopia and Sudan. The Massawans would have traded salt for butter, ivory, hides and so on, and then exported those to the rest of the ancient world.'

He got two more Melottis; after the second they became almost drinkable.

'Some Italian divers recently found a sunken ship off one of the islands,' Cameron said, cracking open the bottles. 'It's quite a fascinating find, really.'

'Ancient?'

'I believe so.'

'Has anyone managed to date it?'

'Roughly.' He frowned. 'The cargo was amphorae of the type used to carry wine, so that must put it before the rise of Islam over in Arabia.'

'Before the seventh century,' I said.

'Yes. I think the ship was trading with the Axumites.'

A different explanation suddenly popped into my mind and I blurted it out. 'Unless they were wine smugglers outrunning Muslim customs officials.'

Cameron gave me another long, hard look.

'Any idea why the ship sank?'

'No,' he said. He took a long sip, the end of the beer bottle disappearing under his beard and coming out again a few inches emptier. 'But I have my own theory,' he said, breathing in deeply. 'The wreck was found off an island which has only one beach. I know – I've been there many times researching the local environment. The waters are quite choppy there at times, when you get a strong wind across the mouth of the Red Sea where it opens up into the Indian Ocean.' His eyes were very still as he spoke, and he didn't blink even once.

'The crew must have been caught in a storm. They saw the beach and decided to head for shelter. That was their last mistake. Unfortunately, there is a reef along the whole length of the beach, about two hundred metres off-shore. The ship hit the reef and sank. If they didn't all drown, then they would have certainly died within a few days. There is no water on the island. No water, no shade, and nothing a human could eat.'

'Their bones are probably still there somewhere,' I said.

'Yes; hard to tell really, there are so many bones around this country.'

That evening Awot was still busy and Cameron had some specimens he had to examine, so I took my chance to explore the old town. The buildings dated back to the Ottoman Empire. They were built of coral rag, with carved doorways and latticed balconies overhanging the street. Missing walls, patched up with rubble, showed a cross-section of house plans.

While Asmara was a European hybrid of Africa and Art Deco, and Keren was a town of villas inhabited by desert dwellers, Massawa smelt of Sinbad and the veiled, doe-eyed daughters of sultans. It had both feet in Arabia as it looked out to sea, but over the centuries it had had cause to cast an occasional apprehensive glance over its shoulder, up into the dark continent of Africa. Especially in the last thirty years, when Eritrean rebels and Ethiopian colonists had done their best to destroy it in their fighting.

Thirty years is very nearly a lifetime in Eritrea, but it is little more than a short hiccup in the lives of places and cities. Massawa had been destroyed before; it had survived the Persian, Roman, Ottoman, Egyptian, Italian and Ethiopian Empires, and would probably survive Eritrea too. The ethnic hotpot of people who had lived in Massawa for generations

Massawa: old bank and governor's palace;
early twentieth century.

had fled abroad, and displaced Afar, and Tigrinya villagers
had moved into the ruins in their stead, but the fragrance of
those days had soaked into the very stones. Despite the
destruction, if you smelt the night breeze you could still get a
whiff of what Massawa had been like.

During the day the sun glared off the whitewashed buildings and everyone was inside asleep, hidden behind shuttered
windows. But when the sun set, the colours seeped back into
the surfaces, as moisture was slowly sucked up from the
ground and people began to wake up and stretch inside their
lattice-shaded rooms. As night thickened the streets were busy
as the locals savoured the night-time cool of thirty-five degrees
and the air was rich with the smells of incense, roasting coffee
and grilled fish.

As the evening call to prayer summoned the faithful to the white stone interior of the main mosque, I felt myself part of a story that started long before the war with Ethiopia, and would continue long past it.

I told Cameron about this feeling.

'Yes, it's a story that is still going on,' he told me. 'Like all good stories, Massawa keeps collecting bits of its history and adding to itself.'

I walked around town, exploring the layers of each conqueror's efforts to stamp their own authority on the town.

There was the old Italian bank, an exhibit of proud colonialism, done up with stucco shells and fish, but now scarred with bullets and shells. It overlooked the quayside where Evelyn Waugh had stepped ashore and begun to batter his Italian escort into giving him a lift up to the highlands.

Saturday 29th August 1936
Heat frightful. Very reluctant sleep there. No telephone. No cars to get to town. At last we found a good-natured captain who was going to station Gura near Asmara. Set out in crowded little car. Magnificent road.

Black and white photos showed the bank in all its glory, when the Askaris paraded in starched uniforms and the Italian officers marched crisply on their boot heels, when Eritrea was part of the second Roman Empire and white men ruled the earth.

Haile Selassie's old seaside palace was a crumbling wreck. Built in 1872 as the Egyptian governor's palace, it was later

Palace ruins: Massawa.

used as the Ethiopian emperor's winter palace. Its domed roof cracked, like a dropped eggshell. It had been looted numerous times and now its insides lay spilt around the courtyard. There were cast-iron bathtubs from Abercrombie and Fitch, smashed fragments of wooden panelling, rubble and furniture. Through the gaping holes you could look up into vaulted chambers, where sea draughts made the mahogany fans swing slowly round and round. The Lions of Judah were still rampant on its iron-grille gates, but there were black crows nesting in the tiled chambers.

The rusty rail track that set off aggressively inland from the end of the causeway was a relic from the second Roman Empire, but since liberation, when the old men had been gathered together to help rebuild it, it was the beginning of a tale about a new-born Africa. Maybe it would be repaired and maybe tourists would come to enjoy the ride. Until then Afar tribesmen sat on its rusty railings and looked down into the bloody water of the Red Sea, watching tropical fish slalom between the needles of sea urchins and the fronds of weeds.

The old maritime culture still survives the demarcation of modern states. Away from the land, where a line is a fixed thing, the local Afar sailors drift between Eritrea, Djibouti and Yemen, trading in fish and televisions. They are a people without a state, drifting between states without a unified people to fill them.

The dhows and local houris emptied their loads of tuna, red snapper and shark each day at the Ministry of Marine Resources. The boats had modern, electric iceboxes inside long planked hulls with crooked masts cut from the local trees. The fishermen were reluctant to come ashore and leave their boats. They sat aft under their awnings of reed mats, only jumping down to weigh their catch or repair their nets. When their business with the ministry was over, they sped back out to sea.

The prostitutes in the bars were left over from the large Ethiopian garrisons. They'd been forced down here by economic hardship to sell their bodies to men who were going to die, but now the war had ended and the men had died. Many of the whores had died as well, of Aids or violence or alcoholism. Now they made better money relieving foreign sailors of their sexual drive and hard currency. I met one, whose tight T-shirt and mini-skirt were an advertiser's dream, who decided I needed company as much as she needed my money.

'I have a girlfriend,' I said, and she lowered her eyes and giggled. She was very pretty, with deep bronze skin and round eyes, and a bunch of dreadlocks pulled back from her face. As she pressed close up to me I could see she wore more gold than clothing.

'I love you.' She breathed the words over me, as warm and soothing as massage oil.

'I'm married,' I replied, and she giggled.

'I'm thirsty,' she smiled in just recognisable English. She giggled, and got herself a bottle of Melotti.

'So when did you come here?' I said, because she obviously was new. Experienced whores didn't bother to waste their time with white foreigners like me: Filipino sailors or Eritreans were the regulars.

'Yesterday,' she said. She shuffled towards me, and there was nothing between me and sin but her blue T-shirt and a dim recollection of something my mother said to me when I was young. She shuffled up to me and I shuffled away.

'Listen, I think you're wasting your time,' I told her.

'Fuck fuck?' she said.

'No fuck,' I told her severely.

She licked her lips and ground her groin into the seat.

'I'm good,' she pouted, and giggled again.

'Fuck fuck,' she pleaded, and ran a fingernail down my thigh.

'Fuck no!' I gasped.

V

'Hello,' the woman said in a musical voice. 'I've been expecting you.'

'You're Ruth?' I asked.

'I am,' Ruth said. 'Come in.'

Ruth was Bilen. She lived in Keren Lalai, a lively suburb of children and animals, with farmyard noises that shook the walls from dawn till dusk. The cocks started it, setting off the donkeys, who brayed themselves breathless and then began again.

I'd been given her address by a friend at the school – no street or number, just descriptions of how to get to her house. At the door of the house I was looking for, four boys were playing with a football made of tightly wrapped plastic bags. They hit each other and cried and made it up again. Two young girls drew circles in the dust, rubbed them out and drew them again. I knocked on the door and listened to footsteps hurrying towards me. I shouted out who I was, and then the lock clicked and the door swung open.

The evening I arrived at her house, Ruth was wearing an embroidered dress. She burnt incense that smelt of churches, conjuring a cloud of white smoke into the room like a witch.

The single forty-watt bulb was so old and dirty that it barely gave off more light than a candle flame. She boiled water as the white cloud of incense drifted through the window and doorway, and then made us cups of sweet tea flavoured with cardamom.

She'd been a fighter, which was where she had met Awot. Ruth had joined the struggle with her sister, who was killed in the Battle of Nakfa. Her father had been in Una, a village near Keren, when the Ethiopian Army rounded up the villagers in the mosque and church and then massacred them by shooting through the windows. They killed seven hundred people in about half an hour. Like many of the other women who joined the struggle, Ruth did not take up arms for lofty ideals like patriotism or a multi-party democracy; she joined for vengeance.

Ruth kept a photo of her dead father and sister on her wall. He was a wild-looking man, with a long ragged afro with a wooden comb thrust into it at an angle. He had the same round eyes and high cheekbones as his daughter. I peered into the face of a dead man and tried to puzzle out who he was. There wasn't much to go on – his features and the enigma of his expression. But what did strike me were his eyes. They were very black and round, and pierced his skull like two bullet-holes.

In the corner of his photo was thrust a passport shot of Ruth's sister. She was a thin-faced girl with shaggy dread-locks and a white, toothy smile from the grave. Her round eyes and high cheekbones made her look like a premonition of her own death, and the skull she now was.

Ruth said that life was hard these days, much harder than in the Field.

'In the Field men and women all shared jobs,' she told me. 'The women did everything men did, including fight. We all lived in fear of death, but we were not afraid of dying for the struggle. Men and women all supported each other. We were fighting for what was right, and the struggle was our immortality.'

'So how has your life changed since liberation?' I asked.

'Now I have my job, and my mother to support, and the children.' She got about a thousand nakfa, US$100, a month. 'But it's not enough,' she said. 'All in all I have eleven people to feed with my single wage, as well as repaying a loan I took out to build my mother a house in Asmara. And I am alone now with my two sons. I have to feed them and cook and send them to school.'

'Where's the father?'

'He was sacrificed in the struggle,' she said, with a soldier's matter-of-factness.

'So do you make your boys help in the housework?' I asked her, curious to see if she still stuck to the idea of equality.

'Yes, of course,' Ruth laughed. 'You know, in the Field we thought that we had changed society. We never thought that after liberation society would change us, but it has. There were only sixty thousand fighters compared to three million civilians. I think all the things we fought for have been forgotten already, except liberation. But what is liberation for women if we are still slaves of the men? We must keep fighting the oppression of women in society. These things will change, but only slowly.'

We sat under a tree, which slowly rained dead leaves on us.

Ruth toasted green coffee beans over a brazier of coals that she fanned to glowing. The beans rattled in the tin till they turned shining black-brown, and gave off the smell of roasted coffee. She pounded them to a powder and boiled them up with root ginger. When the coffee was ready she poured it through a filter of horsehair into small cups half filled with sugar. It was syrupy sweet, and aggressively gingery in the back of the throat.

'I have an aunt in America,' Ruth told me, 'and I asked her to get me a job in the US. Anything. I can work very hard, even if it's a bad job. Then I can send money back to my mother and family. For those people who fled abroad as refugees life is now very good. They are now settled. Especially the ones in Europe or America. They have good lives now, and for us, who risked our lives, what do we have? We are poor still.'

After we drank coffee Ruth took me to see Mama Teka.

Mama Teka was seventy-eight years old, but had the solid bones of a young woman. She had given birth to twelve healthy children, all of whom had survived. Ten of them were abroad, in the USA, Italy, Saudi Arabia, England, Germany, Scandinavia. They had fled Eritrea because the Ethiopians either conscripted young men to fight the EPLF, or shot them as subversives.

'They drove my children away,' Mama Teka complained, 'and they also shot both my dogs!'

Mama Teka had a TV, video, washing machine, gas oven and a car, which was kept under a tarpaulin. Her home compared very favourably with Ruth's single bare room next door.

Noah was one of the two children who had stayed behind in Eritrea. He had a bald patch, and sweated and panted from the effort of moving the weight of his body around. He had been too young to be an EPLF soldier, and the Ethiopians had left him alone. Once he had tried to run away to the Field, but when he got two kilometres outside of town and the world he knew, he started to cry and ran back home before anyone even knew he was missing. He didn't really have what it took to be a fighter. He'd always been a mummy's boy, and had now grown up into a fat mummy's man. Noah lifted the tarpaulin to show me the car. It was a red Ford with patterns of rust and a flat tyre.

'It's good with the girls,' Noah said, as if a knackered old banger with a flat tyre was a Type I Porsche. He grinned at me as he shared his secret. 'I take them out and give them a ride!'

'Yes,' I said, 'I'm sure you do.'

Mama Teka had one other child in Eritrea, a daughter, called Hermon. Hermon was a year younger than Noah, and was also tall and heavily built, but solid, not fat like her brother. Hermon spent her days drinking coffee and plaiting her hair into dreadlocks. She lived for disco and a foreign husband who would come and rescue her from her nationality. Not an Eritrean returnee, she said, but a real, white foreigner.

I met her shade one night on the way to a concert.

'Disco!?' she invited, and her shadow did a little wiggle.

'Disco!' I said.

After the disco we went back and Mama Teka put on a Hindi movie. Behind us on the wall was a cheap tapestry of Jesus with a shining heart and an assortment of holes in his body held up for everyone to see. After half an hour, maybe more, Mama Teka turned to me and asked, 'Can you understand Hindi?'

'No,' I said. 'Can you?'

'No,' she said, shaking her head.

Mama Teka baking flat bread.

We carried on watching the film and got increasingly
bored. Mama Teka told Noah to put on another video. He
heaved himself up and lumbered over to change the tape.

The next one showed the graduation ceremony of one of
her sons in Nottingham, England. 'Biniam Awot,' intoned the
clerk's voice. 'Two one in Computer Science.' There were
shots of Sherwood Forest and a man dressed as Robin Hood,
and then close-ups of Nottingham streets.

The next video showed one of Mama Teka's sons in the
USA. It was Christmastide. 'Yohannes,' Mama Teka told me,
smiling.

Yohannes's house in the US, with a picture by Monet on the
wall, wall-to-wall carpet and Ikea furniture, looked strange,
even to me. In the video Yohannes balanced his two infant

sons on his stomach. He talked in English; Mama Teka didn't understand, but was rapt. Yohannes kept chatting about shopping and the price of the carpet, as his wife filmed. Mama Teka smiled and beamed with pleasure. The video was a postcard from the future, watching her grown-up children whose lives came in ninety-minute instalments – Biniam in the UK, Yohannes in the US, Freweini and Aster in Italy.

As we got up to leave Noah wobbled over to put on some footage of the war. Many of the young men liked to watch war home movies. This one was footage of EPLF soldiers ambushing some Ethiopians. It was hard to see who the fighters were shooting at, but their shouts and behaviour were of people under fire. Their voices and movements were electric with adrenalin and people were dying on screen. For real.

I came out of class one day and found a message from the school secretary that Awot had phoned. He was in town for a meeting: we should meet up at Arregai's later on for dinner.

All the students were filed out of class into line before the flagpole. For the first year the school had not been able to afford a flag, so the raising and lowering were mimed. The second year there began with the announcement from Igzaw that he had bought the school a flag.

It flapped stiff in the wind as it was lowered and the students sang the Eritrean national anthem. They sang in Tigrinya, although there were versions for each of the languages. It was supposed to be full of the song of battle and nationalism, but I'd never learnt the words. I sang along as much as I knew: 'Eritrea, Eritrea, Eritrea – bom-di-bom-di-bom-di-bom . . .'

Walking back, I asked another of the teachers to tell me what the words meant.

'I've no idea,' he said. 'It's all about fighting and the Field. I don't know the words. It's all rubbish.'

Awot was at Arregai's already when I got there, sitting on the veranda, chewing his lip. The sun had set, the streets were busy with men walking back from evening prayers. The waiter brought a pair of cappuccinos and we sat and chatted, but I could tell Awot was only half in the conversation. After a long pause I asked, 'How was the meeting?'

Awot shook his head. Eventually he spoke. 'You know, things are not easy in peacetime. The problem with Eritrea now is that the Ethiopians created a dependency culture; the people daren't do anything themselves.

'The people ask, "Why doesn't the government build us schools or factories, roads or hospitals? Why doesn't the government do this or that?" And do you know what the government says? "Who is going to give you a hospital? If you want a hospital you should build it yourselves." They are trying to make the people responsible for themselves.'

'And is it working?' I asked him.

'It is working,' Awot said, but he didn't sound definite. He put his cup back on to the saucer, sat forward. 'We have to educate them. If they want democracy then they must learn to be responsible for themselves first. They complain that there is no democracy. But democracy is not like a gift. You cannot give someone democracy for Christmas and let them unwrap it. They have to work for it themselves. But it is difficult,' he said, and shook his head. 'We are having problems.'

It seemed that authority had strait-jacketed the EPLF. It would not be the first successful rebel movement to be conquered by victory.

Awot shook his head again. 'I think we are not able to run the country the way we dreamt we would do.'

One afternoon, after I'd finished teaching, I went around to Habtewolde's house, at the end of the row of teacher shacks. He had two rooms: one he shared with his wife and child, the other he used as his studio. He took me in there and he and I sat on the floor.

'Welcome to my floor!' he announced.

'Thank you,' I told him. 'You have the nicest floor I know.'

Habtewolde laughed and clapped his hands together.

'My house is your house,' he replied. 'My floor is your floor.'

'You are too kind.'

Habtewolde had a toddler's view of the world. For him everything was still fresh and exciting; even sitting on the floor made him happy. Sitting cross-legged made him even more happy.

'This is Arabic style,' he laughed. 'Tigrinya do not sit cross-legged, they' – not 'we' – 'squat.'

Habtewolde was a Tigrinya, but he was also a fighter, which made him different: he appreciated the world outside the close confines of his tribal culture.

Fighters were actually a tribe of their own – they had their own culture separate from other Eritreans, their own slang and history in the Field. It was ironic that having fought against the Ethiopians for a united Eritrea, the EPLF then began Eritrea's first years of freedom by creating a new division – not only between the nine ethnic groups, but also between the nine ethnic groups and the fighters. All the best jobs were reserved for fighters. They were now the ruling elite.

Habtewolde was ferociously good-looking, with brown skin and amber eyes, and a black moustache on a gaunt face. He was also a man of violent mood swings – compulsive, creative and destructive; compassionate and cruel by turns. He was a war in himself.

But he was always sincere, and after a little time of sitting there chatting he took my hand and grinned.

'You must come and visit my village,' he said. 'I can take you to kill a goat.' He nodded enthusiastically; I smiled.

'What's your village called?'

'Hadish Adi,' he said.

'Sounds good. When do we go?'

'Tomorrow?' he suggested.

'OK,' I said. 'Tomorrow!'

———

Hadish Adi was about thirty-five kilometres from Keren. The name meant 'New Village', but it had been there for as long as anyone could remember. Yet it must have been new once: it was a frontier settlement, at the furthest limits of traditional Tigrinya land, and built on the top of a mountain for protection against the Bilen.

We set off by minibus in the early morning, as the sun melted the icy black night sky into daylight. After forty minutes we climbed out and began the three-hour walk from the Asmara–Keren highway, along a dust track that meandered around the slopes of the mountainsides. It was a blasted landscape of rocks that were slowly turning to glass under the heat of the sun, whose light ricocheted off the barren slopes into our faces.

Habtewolde devoured the miles with rapacious strides, taking short-cuts down the rocky hillsides with the speed and agility of a goat. I managed to keep up, but lacked his finesse. This was his home soil; he had carried a Kalashnikov for a decade to make it his.

'Are we nearly there?' I asked when we stopped for a break.

'Nearly,' Habtewolde said.

I drank while he just stood, not even looking tired.

'Water?' I offered.

He shook his head. We had plenty to spare, but in his mind he was back in the Field, on a forced march or competing with the other fighters in feats of endurance. We set off again, and after another hour we rounded a corner and saw his village perched on a ridge on the other side of a dry gully. The road snaked down across the dried watercourse and then up and around the bottom of a mound that was halfway up the slopes to the village.

The mound was the Martyrs' Cemetery, where all the fighters who'd died around the village were buried. During the revolution there had been countless small fights, between patrols or spies in the area, low-scale combat which claimed the lives of eighty-six resistance fighters. Their contribution to Eritrea's freedom was marked with a simple concrete monument shaped like the fluted tail of a bomb. Around the edifice there were a thousand yellow desert flowers.

Habtewolde was very close to God. God sent him dreams during the night, and even answered his prayers for rain. His spirituality was part of living so long in the Field with Death holding his hand. Habtewolde stopped and looked at the Martyrs' Cemetery.

'Flowers!' he exclaimed. 'They are a miracle!'

And he was serious.

The first night in Hadish Adi, Habtewolde and I sat in the yard of his family's house, a stone building with great irregular beams holding up a flat roof of many layers of branches mixed with turf.

'This is the same sort of house that Jesus lived in,' Habtewolde said as we sat on reed mats outside. 'I saw a picture in a book once, and it was the same.'

As we talked the day shrank to a rind of turquoise along the horizon. The colour drained down the funnel of the sunset, and the stars came out on a coal-black background, large and white and beaming: not a paltry twinkle in sight.

'Do you know how many Ethiopians were killed around here?' I asked Habtewolde.

'I don't know,' he said, and his mood changed in an instant. He sat pensively, looking away up the hillside. I could guess what he was thinking about.

When Habtewolde was eight years old the Ethiopians came to attack Hadish Adi. They had come from Asmara, destroying each village on the way. Habtewolde stood and watched them burn the village – houses, church, grain stores – to the ground. The villagers stood and watched and wept from a point not two kilometres away, but the Ethiopians did not try to attack them. They were afraid of ambush.

The Ethiopian conscripts slaughtered the cows and goats, burnt the thatch, and drove their tanks through the walls of the houses till all that was left were crumpled shells of buildings, like eggshells after all the liquid has been poured out.

The attack was part of an organised campaign of terror designed to bludgeon the Eritrean people into submission.

When the Tigrinya villagers saw their houses and livelihoods destroyed, they thought of trying to survive in this country without food and shelter. Without grain or their goats they would be hunted by hunger, till starvation came to pick them off, one by one, the weak first, and then the strong. They contemplated their families and how few of them would be alive in a year's time. It was impossible, and they broke down. When the Tigre and Bilen fighters of the ELF saw the Tigrinya villagers weeping, they were angry.

'Why are you crying?' they demanded. 'The Ethiopians have only destroyed your village. Where we are from they also killed our families.' It was true, but not very constructive.

'Their attitude explained why the ELF never succeeded: they were still a tribally based organisation. They never rose above their tribal identity,' Habtewolde told me. 'When I was fourteen I walked from my house to join the struggle. I didn't join the ELF because I wanted to fight for *all* of Eritrea. That group was called the EPLF.'

As Habtewolde and I talked, the evening moved through into night. The hundreds of flowers nodded gently on the bones of the martyrs, and above our heads the stars revolved around the dark.

'I grew up in the Field,' Habtewolde said. 'Like all the young children who joined the EPLF, I was educated in the Revolutionary School.'

When you'd been in Eritrea a little while you learnt to tell the difference between fighters and civilians. All fighters of a certain age were Revolutionary School students, graduates of the classes that Awot had taught, under rocks or trees, or in tunnels in cliffsides. What marked the Revolutionary School graduates out was the fact that they were all outspoken. They were also short, because there was never enough food to eat.

'We didn't even have shoes for our feet,' Habtewolde said, 'but nobody complained. We were always happy.'

Habtewolde had spent the earliest days of his childhood herding goats around the slopes of Hadish Adi. Each day he took them high up into the hills. It was a lonely job for a small child, with no food or water, and the fear of snakes or lions to torment the imaginative mind. The isolation made Habtewolde deeply religious. He believed that God protected him from animals in the wilderness, as he had protected Jesus for forty days and nights in the desert. God had also protected Habtewolde from the bombs and guns of the Ethiopians.

But this religious devotion was not approved of in the Field. The EPLF was a Communist organisation. They wanted to wipe away traces of tribe and religion, to make all their conscripts the same as each other – simply fighters. Fighters were not Muslim or Christian, or Tigre or Tigrinya or Afar or Bilen; they were soldiers who were fighting for the liberation of Eritrea from the Ethiopians. And from ethnicity.

'They used to call me a savage because I was poor and religious. But I never listened to them,' Habtewolde said. 'I am proud of my faith.'

Habtewolde wrote poetry. Like Wordsworth, nature inspired him to words, especially sunsets, mornings, stars and birds. He told me that in the Field he used to lie and stare up at the poor man's ceiling – the sky – and dream about peace. He'd grown up with the war in the same way that I'd grown up with pop music. The war was older than he was, like an older brother it had always been there.

Habtewolde read me a short story he'd written. He translated from the Tigrinya:

A girl was farming. The sun was hot and the ground was stony, but she kept looking up for the sound or sight of Ethiopian aircraft. She was very frightened of them because she had seen people dying in a napalm attack. Her parents had been killed in a napalm attack on her village.

The girl had been working all day, since before dawn, first cooking food for her friends and then helping in the fields. The week before, she had been caring for wounded soldiers, and she might be doing the same the next week. Or she might be a soldier herself, with a Kalashnikov and a string of bullets, and a row of men to shoot.

As she farmed she heard a voice calling, 'Daughter, my daughter!' and suddenly she looked up like she was receiving a telephone call from God. At that moment she wanted to fly to the G7 summit or to the UN conference, or the flower-filled gardens of the rich, and tell them that she would only die once, but that they would die twice.

It was a parable which made him laugh, the chuckle of the Grim Reaper waiting in the shadows.

'I have always been a poor man,' he explained, 'so I will reach the kingdom of heaven. But the G7, the UN – the rich – won't. The girl in the story is a fighter. She wants the powerful people of the world to stop the war in Eritrea. But they don't. They only want to make themselves richer. She wants to tell them that she will reach the kingdom of heaven, but that they will not. They will die twice.' Habtewolde laughed again, and his lips peeled back into a broad white smile.

About a month later, I met Habtewolde coming out of his class. We walked back to his room for bread and tea.

'Come here!' he said, when we were at his doorway. 'But first you must close your eyes!'

I did. He took my hand softly and led me into the room.

I heard him strike matches in the darkness.

'Open them,' he said, his voice close. I opened my eyes.

The room was dark, except for a table dressed up like an altar, with four lit candles that cast little pools of yellow light. Above it was a watercolour painting of a dove, and the words THE BLOOMING DAY OF OUR FRIENDSHIP.

On the table was a plastic statue of St Anthony, and clay statues of birds that Habtewolde had crafted and coloured in bright enamel paints. He lifted the clay statues with extraordinary care and tenderness, as if they were living animals. 'I have made an exhibition,' he said, stroking a two-kilogram, glossy grey pigeon. 'I hope to raise enough money to go to Norway and show my birds. I have a friend there.' He put the pigeon down next to its wife and put some rice down for them to eat. Then he lifted a red enamel bird with blue, human eyes and a black beak and cooed at it.

'I want to show the Norwegian people my birds,' he looked up and said. 'Eritrea has good relations with Norway. Even in the Field. When I was in the Revolutionary School we had biscuits we used to call "Norway". They came during the famine.

The boxes they came in had the word "Norway" on them. That's why we called them "Norway". We had no idea it was the name of a country. What did we know? We only knew the war. We used to say to each other, "Have you got any Norways?" "No, not today." There were three biscuits: salt, sugar and glucose. If you ate all three with a little water then you could go for two or three days without feeling hungry. We also had biscuits called "Oxfam". But they weren't so nice.'

'I thought the EPLF didn't get food aid during the war. Did you capture it from the Ethiopians?'

Habtewolde cradled the bird in his hand and sat down. 'We were given food, but to be truthful it was for the people who lived under the protection of the fighters. But they wanted to share it with us. Some was also given for the Ethiopian POWs. They ate better than we did, so sometimes we stole from them, because we were so hungry. We had nothing to eat. Then there would be an announcement to collect all the aid packages. This happened when a foreign monitor was coming. We would all go running around and pick up all the tins.'

We sat in silence surrounded by his birds as the candle flames danced.

'I think we'll have to go back to my village,' he said suddenly.

'OK,' I said. 'How about the day after tomorrow?'

'I'm preaching then. But the day after the day after tomorrow?'

'It's agreed.'

'Good,' he said without elaborating. 'I want to take you to the Fairy Caves.'

We set off before dawn, walking through the stony landscape towards his village. I tried to imagine fairies in such a landscape, but couldn't. Fairies dance near quiet grassy streams, or in the evening damp of forests, soft, magical places of plants and animals. Deserts couldn't have fairies, only the ghosts of fairies: hard, excessive spirits like the djinn, or the desert storm.

We slept at his father's house, and next morning Habtewolde was dressed for a beach party, in Bermuda shorts, T-shirt and a wide-brimmed straw hat. I wore shades, desert boots, long safari shorts and a T-shirt. Habtewolde gave me his hat to wear.

'You'll need it,' I said to him.

'I was a fighter,' he told me.

I remembered the shadeless walk to Habtewolde's village, and relented. 'OK,' I said. 'Give me the hat.'

We set off in the cool half-hour before dawn. As we walked the midnight sky paled to indigo, and a strip of turquoise began to glow along the eastern horizon, like the inside of a Turkish palace. We trudged on through the early morning, passing shrouded figures going in the opposite direction, on their way to a scene in the Old Testament, or back to the Underworld. Habtewolde spoke only once: 'This land invites you to dream, not speak.'

The light slowly spread across the sky like bleach, and when we stopped to rest the air was a pale blue. The temperature was still cool, but the first touch of the sun was like the early stirrings of a furnace. Habtewolde leapt ahead, going from rock to rock, and pulled a radio out of his rucksack. It was tuned in to the BBC World Service. The news from London was of other people's wars. Details of deaths and damage pursued us through the air like banshees.

The path lulled our senses in a citrus orchard of yellow

blossoms, and then tried to torment us as it climbed through bare hillsides covered with stones that reflected the sunlight up into our faces. Around mid-morning we walked above a gorge where a river had once churned its way. Tributary gullies flowed in from either side, and when we crossed over them we saw the hot stones had been worn smooth by water. But now the river and tributaries were all dry and echoing.

We stopped for a drink and all I could hear was the gentle whisper of the wind. I imagined the torrents that had carved scars in the mountainsides when this land was still Eden. But when we set off walking again there was only the clatter of loose stones. We passed dead baobab trees, rigid scarecrows to warn off the living. The rocks pushed their way through the dried, peeling skin of topsoil like old bones. The loss of life in the war was even more wasteful when you saw that they had all died for a land that was dead.

We walked under Monkey Rock, a hump of bare rock with jagged sides, and then crossed the main riverbed.

'Do monkeys still live there?' I asked.

'I have seen baboons there,' he said, looking up as if he might catch a glimpse of them, 'but the droughts killed most of them off. And then the Ethiopians shot them.'

We came down a ridge and found a leaking irrigation pipe pumping water to a field. A young girl was filling a bucket from the trickle that splashed down. A scintillating cloud of yellow butterflies, attracted by the water, formed a halo around her head. We stopped again to rest and I drank some water. Habtewolde ruffled the girl's dreadlocks, and then asked her name. I had students who names meant 'Victory' or 'Freedom', but I'd never heard her name before.

Caves of the Fairy King.

Habtewolde ruffled her hair as if giving her a blessing: 'She said her name was Peace,' he smiled.

The river was broad at this point, with a staircase of rock that would have been a tumbling waterfall if there was water. Habtewolde announced that we had reached the Halls of the Fairy King.

The King held court in the maze of smooth-walled caves nibbled through the waterfall. There were tunnels and gullies, and rock-pools of cool water that lingered in the deeper caves left over from last year's rains.

We went skinny-dipping.

'I used to play here when I was a boy,' Habtewolde said as we splashed. 'I haven't been back for fifteen years. Since before I went to join the Field.'

We wallowed in the cool water, then Habtewolde suddenly leapt up and went chasing off down a tunnel. He shouted and whooped and called back, 'I've seen the King of the Fairies!'

There was more splashing.

'Can you hear his music?'

Then, 'Follow me!'

I did not hear the Fairy King's music and he did not leave footprints – but Habtewolde did, neat prints in the soft wet sand, and his laughing voice echoed through the stone. I set off after him, going deeper and deeper through pools and tunnels and over stones smooth as silk. Then I was in a wide pool of chilling water that dripped from a stone roof, and I couldn't tell which way he'd taken. His voice came from all directions at once. I swam for a while and listened to his echoes, then found a different way up into the daylight.

Habtewolde was outside, looking lost and bewildered. He waited aimlessly while I rubbed down my white limbs. He had stopped talking about the Fairy King.

'Time for lunch,' he said.

We sat down to eat bread and bananas and roasted barley flour in a pool of shade under a baobab. Habtewolde broke the bread and offered it to me, and then mixed flour with sugar and water and gave it to me to drink. He didn't eat or drink, as if he could survive on just watching.

'You should eat,' I told him, 'or at least drink.'

He didn't answer, just turned his amber eyes down. He was strikingly handsome.

'Are you OK, Habtewolde?' I asked him.

His mind was in the depths of the caves. It wasn't the Fairy King that had lured him through the halls, but the spirit of himself as a boy, before he left to join the struggle, and the spirits of other boys, now bones under the flowers on the martyrs' graves. I couldn't find anything to say to him.

He said he was going for a walk.

He came back after a long time, lay down on the rock and closed his eyes.

————

A couple of weeks later Habtewolde winced as he took me into a local Keren beer bar.

An old hag revealed her last tooth as we stood in the door-way. 'Come in,' she motioned.

A sweet-faced young girl in a mini-skirt and a tight white T-shirt came up to us and spoke to Habtewolde in an unfriendly voice, but he ignored her. This wasn't the place a devout Christian should be in and he was quickly searching the room with his eyes. Habtewolde looked relieved when he found the man he was looking for, a short, plump fighter who had been his best friend in the Field. His friend was called Adam, and Adam was religiously drunk.

'He saved my life in the Field,' Habtewolde briefed me as we walked over, 'and I want to save his soul.'

We joined Adam, who ordered us two cups of the local beer, which was called sewer. It was an apt name for a drink in which lumps of yeast fizzed in a surface scum, then slowly sank to the bottom of the glass to congeal in clots.

'We were Revolutionary School students together,' Habtewolde said, half to me and half to Adam; 'we were called "the Spearhead". We were very special for when liber-ation came. We were always told that we would spearhead the social changes in Eritrea. If we are to keep up that force we must continue in our dedication. We must continue to meet and discuss. If we spend our time drinking and smoking and being immoral then we will lose our power.'

Adam ignored Habtewolde completely; I guess he'd heard it all before. He sat, wobbling slightly with inebriation, watching me, and waiting for Habtewolde to stop so that he could speak. Habtewolde did.

'We cannot go back to the Field,' Adam said, 'the lives we lived there! We were children shoved inside a box. We were in a box inside a box. We were not allowed to even have girl-friends or boyfriends. We had to devote ourselves to the struggle. One hundred per cent! The life we had there we cannot continue.'

'But there is no learning from mistakes with HIV. If you make that mistake then you kill yourself,' Habtewolde said suddenly.

'Don't worry. There is a hundred per cent chance of me not having that problem,' Adam declared, and drank more sewer.

Habtewolde suddenly stood up and left. The mood just took him. Adam went to piss outside in the street, and as I waited I watched a man peel the young girl's tight T-shirt up over her breasts and then take her into a side room. Adam's drinking mate, an old befuddled man with a thin moustache and pierced ear, embraced me and poured his beery breath down my neck.

'Many young fighters have many problems,' he told me, as if he didn't. 'Some have a good lifestyle but others find it very difficult. They were taught in the war to be fighters. Their teachers were fighters and everyone they knew were fighters and fighting and the struggle was all that they knew. Just fighters, you see. Now they have money they spend it on drink and cigarettes and women.' He shook his head, and held his mug of sewer like it might escape if he didn't keep an eye on it. He opened his mouth again, but forgot what he was going to say, and sat opened-mouthed with a look of shock.

'So why are you drinking here?'

'I've got no job.'

'It's difficult to find work,' I sympathised.

'No. I don't like work.'

'Who does?'

'I mean I don't work. I refuse.'

'So where does your money come from?'

'I have relatives abroad,' he said.

'Where are they?'

'Saudi. But it's very hard there. They're not allowed to hold Christian ceremonies. All their weddings and christenings are in secret.'

'Why don't they come back to Eritrea then?'

'They won't get a job.'

'They don't like work either?'

'No, they're not fighters.'

'I see,' I said.

The man leant in close to me. 'There's only one person in the country who knows what's happening,' he said. 'That's the President. He just tells his men what to do and they follow blindly. It's like one man trying to teach the whole country how to read and write. We don't want that. We want democracy.'

'So what should the government do?'

'They should give more jobs to civilians,' he said. 'The people are tired of soldiers in this country. Soldiers only know how to do one thing. Fight.'

Adam came back. Meeting me seemed to have twigged something in his brain.

'You're from England?' he asked. I nodded. 'I am a supporter of Tony Blair,' he announced. 'I like Tony Blair and the Labour Party leader before him.'

'John Smith?'

'Before him.'

'Neil Kinnock.'

'Yes – Neil Kinnock.' Adam belched. 'What's his wife's name?'

'Glenys,' I said.

'Yes, Glenys came to visit the Field in 1989.' Adam smiled. 'When I was in the Revolutionary School, in grade seven. I met her. I shook her hand. When she visited the trenches and wrote a book about us fighters, we thought that would be the end of the war.'

'Ah,' I said while Adam drank. 'What was your job in the Field? Did you actually fight?'

'I was a teacher,' Adam said. 'My school was twenty minutes from the front-line trenches. One night the Ethiopians attacked. It was very terrible. Every man for himself; many of our fighters were sacrificed. Terrible!'

'So is it better being a civilian than being in the Field?'

'Yes! When I came to Keren I handed in my gun. I gave it to the police. I said, "I don't want to even see a gun again." Today – did you hear? – there was a gun practice behind the hills. All the people got excited and said it was the Sudanese invading. I didn't even want to hear it. Not even the sound of guns. Nothing!

'Have some sewer,' he said.

'Is there anything else?'

'No.'

'Just a bit then.'

Adam ordered another round. He refused to let me pay.

'So what will you do with yourself; will you stay as a teacher?' I asked him.

'I want to write,' he said.

I'd seen a couple of books by Eritrean writers: they had garish covers and showed lovers or soldiers or both.

'Is it difficult to get stuff published in Eritrea?' I asked.

'Quite. Everything must be submitted to the ministry. They decide if it will be published or not. It is lucky for me that I am a fighter: I know their sickness. They want stories about the struggle.'

'So you can start writing then!'

'How? You live in the struggle, but how can you write? If I write then maybe I will write about some secret. No! the people at the top should write first, then the rest of us will know about what we can write,' he told me. Then, with a flourish of double logic, he looked at me and said, 'When the government tells us what we are allowed to say, only then we can write.'

VI

One night I walked home through the moonlit streets and fell in with an Eritrean going the same way.

'Hi, man!' he said. 'I'm from Washington DC. How do you like my country?'

We moved together through the moon shadows, walking side by side.

'It's good,' I said.

He thanked me, and then there was a moment's silence.

'Has Eritrea changed much since you were last here?'

'Yes. It's nice now,' he told me. 'When I left, the Ethiopians were killing men my age.'

The man's name was Kesete. He planned to retire here – when the kids grew up, that was; they couldn't come here because they were American.

'How do you find America?' I asked.

'I like Washington, man. But it's too cold now; it's below zero. But my family is there. Your home is where the heart is. You should see my son. He plays basketball. He's eleven years old and six foot four. It's sweet, I tell you.'

We came to a street where the whores sat in their doorways, sifting through the drunken debris of the night.

'Sorry,' I said, 'I go this way.'

'OK, man. Nice to have met you,' he said and walked on up the road. I went on a few streets in the darkness when I saw ahead a single man standing in the middle of the deserted street. It was like he'd been waiting for me, or that we'd always been destined to meet here, just that I'd never known.

He didn't speak as I came closer, which added to the night-time air of expectancy. I stopped five paces from him, till I could see the streetlight reflected in the convexity of his eye-balls. We stood. I could hear his breathing. Then he dropped his trousers to show me his genitalia, which peeked modestly out from under his flapping shirt.

I walked past him, but a few paces on I heard him turn to follow me, shuffling along with his trousers round his ankles. There was a prickle of fear down my spine.

I began to run.

He ran too.

He grabbed a wheelbarrow and chased me – shuffling, rattling and moaning. I leapt up my steps and fumbled at the lock, and ducked through just in time. I peered out to see him sweep on under the moon, with his wheelbarrow, a spectre of death taking souls to hell.

———

Dawit was short and broad. He had a handsome face, with piercing hazel eyes and a pencil-thin goatee drawn over his chin. He was also a teacher at the school, and lived next door to Habtewolde. Both of them were fighters, but that was where the similarities ended.

For a start, Dawit was not a religious man like Habtewolde. 'I cannot spend all my evenings praying,' he told me.

Habtewolde said Dawit led a dissolute life, consorting with 'rubbish', 'gamblers' and 'prostitutes'. From the moral heights that Habtewolde commanded this could mean almost half of Eritrean society. But Dawit *did* have a seedy streak, an aimlessness that came from having lost faith in anything but his own future.

I asked Dawit how he had joined the EPLF as a child. He picked up the grade-seven English textbook and read out a passage about people walking to join the Field through the enemy lines in a bored voice:

> Travelling to the liberated areas was not easy. Many
> people used overgrown narrow paths and abandoned
> roads to avoid the danger of falling into enemy hands.
> These trails were often difficult on foot and impossible
> by any other means. The escapees never used the main
> roads, of course. They travelled on foot for days and
> nights with little food or water and no help. They all
> had to use the same unknown, rough and painful routes.

'It was just like that,' he said.

One Friday afternoon Dawit was sitting on a rock under the school wall. We sat in the shade, overseeing the students: Muslim girls in skirts and thick leggings were skipping and playing volleyball; boys were heading for the ruins of an Ethiopian guardhouse which was now the school teahouse.

In front of us the slope dipped into the valley, and then climbed steeply up the tallest of the mountains surrounding

Keren: Lalumba, Bilen for 'Forested Crown'. There were no trees now, and its rocky crags looked steel-blue in the sunlight. White clouds had drifted in during the afternoon, and floated around looking lost. Some had run aground on Lalumba's crags.

'I have been up there,' Dawit said, nodding towards Lalumba and rattling stones in his fist.

'Can you climb it?'

'No,' he said: 'there are landmines. The Ethiopians used to have trenches up at the top.' Dawit sat in silence and after a while he nodded his head up towards the cloud-wreathed summit of Lalumba. 'Just after liberation I carried a man down from there,' Dawit said. 'He was blown up by a landmine.'

'Did you know him?'

'Oh yes. He was a fighter, like me. We were not friends, but I knew him in the Field.' Dawit paused. 'It was just after liberation and he'd come back to see his family. After it happened his family was too frightened to go and help him. I was a fighter and there was another fighter who needed help. I went into the minefield and got him out. He was still talking when I found him, but as we came down his face got whiter and whiter. Well, I knew from the Field. His mother and father were talking to him all the way down, asking him if he was all right – they thought he was still alive. So we took him to the hospital and there they said he was dead.'

We sat in silence for a few minutes, Dawit rattling the pebbles in his hand, me just sitting and thinking.

'It was trench warfare, wasn't it?' I asked.

'Yes,' he nodded.

I thought of the First World War and the trenches there.

Dawit continued rattling pebbles in his fist. 'The trenches ran from here all the way to the Red Sea.'

'Sometimes it sounds more like a guerrilla war.'

'It was that as well. The problem was that we didn't have any aircraft.'

I watched the children in front of us playing in their morning break.

'What do you think of the students?' I asked.

'Huh!' he responded.

Dawit had been a teacher in the Field, and after liberation he had been forced to continue teaching. He had no choice, until he was discharged from the Army. He tossed his pebbles against a rock some feet away. 'I don't like teaching here,' he told me in a flat voice. 'In the Field teaching was different. The students now are not the same. I was a fighter, not a teacher. My vocation is not teaching. I joined the EPLF because it was a revolution. Everyone was working to defeat the enemy. Now there is no enemy. We have won, but I am still not free.'

'Why don't you just leave?'

'I can't. I'm still a fighter. If I refuse to teach I will be arrested and court-martialled.' Dawit turned and smiled. 'Maybe you can find me an English girl, then I can go to England.'

'You want to go to England?'

'I don't care where I go,' he said.

'But what about Eritrea?'

'Who cares about Eritrea.'

The more time I spent with ex-fighters like Habtewolde, Adam and Dawit, the more I could see that the cement of the revolution was crumbling. The dreams of liberation were turning sour. Liberation and peace had been the Promised Land for so long, the reality could never live up to thirty years of expectations.

The disappointment was especially noticeable in the fighters. Men and women who had risked life for liberation, who had watched their friends and comrades die. The few fighters who had jobs in the ministries were still loyal, but those outside were realising that they were on their own now. Some were turning to religion, some to drink, others in to themselves.

I wondered whether Dawit would pull a dying man from a minefield now, or not. I thought not.

———————

The Grand Hotel had been the US Army's recreation centre for weekends away from their radio base at Kagnew Station. Now it was Keren's main sports centre. Weeds rampaged through the concrete of the basketball court; the swimming pool was empty; plaster hung off the walls like ripped wall-paper. The whole place felt like the ruins of some civilisation that had retreated from a border outpost.

One day after school I was playing basketball when I turned and saw a white man watching the game. He was tall and fat with a mournful expression. If he'd been a stray dog you would have wanted to take him in and give him a biscuit.

I stopped playing and went over for a chat. When I came close I saw that he had a very close-cut beard, small watery blue eyes and heavy, Goofy jowls. We shook hands and he told me he was from a small town in Ohio. His town had the best girls' basketball team in the state. There were two eleven-year-olds who were both six foot three.

'Do they eat fertiliser for breakfast?' I asked.

'I don't know what they do, but they sure do it well,' he answered without a smile.

We looked at each other, maybe a little confused. I smiled again. He didn't respond.

'Did you know that this used to be a US Army base?' he asked at last.

'Yes,' I said. 'Were you here?'

'I came. This place was just a weekend resort. I was in Kagnew Station in Asmara. The whole place is a bit more run-down now. Not so much damage as in Massawa, though.'

We stopped and thought of what to say.

'Yes,' I said at last. 'They made a mess of Massawa.'

'They sure did.' He continued looking at nothing in particular. 'They sure did.'

I waited. He turned to face me and his eyes focused slowly. 'Well, nice to meet you.' He gave me his hand to shake. It was soft and small, almost feminine.

I said, 'Bye,' and watched him walk off into the Keren evening, looking for something or someone that wasn't there any more.

———

Habtewolde was rushing about with a poem buzzing inside him like a bee. He couldn't talk: God had telephoned at last. I was left looking at his closed door, and him running off.

'Have you met Tedros?' he shouted over his shoulder.

'Who?' I shouted.

'A new teacher – next door!' his voice drifted back to me as he dashed off.

I looked at Habtewolde's locked door and saw that, along the row of rooms, the door next to his was ajar. I knocked on it and peered in. On the bed on the left I saw a pair of feet and a book. The feet got up, and two hands rubbed two bleary eyes.

'I'm Tedros,' the man said. He put down the book he was reading. The title was *How to Create Miracles in Your Everyday Life*. Tedros saw me read the title. 'Oh, I am not a spiritualist,' he said, 'but I am spiritual. I think there is a difference, no?' His voice was soft and gentle.

We shook hands.

Tedros was a fighter. I knew straight away. But he wasn't of the same generation as Habtewolde or Dawit. He hadn't been a Revolutionary School student, he didn't have their dwarfish stature, and there was a thoughtfulness to him the younger fighters did not have. They'd been indoctrinated as children to fight for liberation and Marxism and the EPLF; Tedros didn't have their black-and-white view of the world. He'd joined the struggle as a young man. For him it was a conscious decision, to risk his life for the chance of liberating Eritrea. I asked him about it.

'I was too old for the Revolutionary School,' Tedros told me softly; 'they only wanted young children.' His eyes were very wide, as if he was startled, but his voice had a soft, soothing touch, like a healer's. It was a religious voice. He could have done the voice-over on a cartoon for the character of God. Not the dictatorial words of the Old Testament, 'I am the LORD,' but the gentle God of the New Testament who said, 'Treat your brother as you would be treated yourself.' 'When I was a boy at school I always wanted to be a teacher,' he said. 'Then there were only two professions in the country, teacher and doctor.'

One Friday Tedros and I sat overlooking the town. It was a hot morning with bright white clouds and a bright blue sky that was too colourful to be real. The students were all in class studying, and the air was very still and very hot, but as we sat through till mid-afternoon the long bright sunlight boiled up storms of clouds on the horizon.

I was looking at the shanty town on the edge of Keren and thinking of the EPLF's promises of oil and precious minerals when liberation came. Was there really anything worth mining under the dry earth and impoverished housing? I thought about England and the Industrial Revolution, and how Britain became rich.

'Is there any coal in Eritrea?' I asked Tedros suddenly. He was a geography teacher, so I guessed he'd know.

'No,' Tedros said softly and sincerely and with the reverence of a churchgoer.

We watched the wind whip up great swirling columns of dust. The distant clouds bubbled up into mountains in the blue sky.

'Is it true that there was a lot of coal in Britain but that now it has all gone?' he asked in return.

'The coal near the surface has all gone. They dig deep down now. Sometimes they dig under the sea.'

'Coal is a very cheap energy, isn't it?'

'Yes, but it causes acid rain.'

'So it is true!' he whispered. 'Sulphur turns to acid rain and kills the trees. I have also heard that it kills fish. Is it so?'

'I think so,' I said, and Tedros nodded in wonder.

We sat in silence.

The wind kept swirling around the bowl of Keren.

The topsoil blew with it.

'Tell me. Do you think the soil here is good?' Tedros asked me.

'It looks good. If only there was some water.'

'Yes, water,' he said, and there was a long pause. 'Which is better, brown soil or yellow soil, do you think?'

'I always thought yellow soil was better,' I told him. 'In China they have a soil called loess, which is yellow. It's metres deep, twenty metres or more, and it is very fine. When it rains the soil becomes like clay. That is very good soil.'

'You know, in Eritrea there is a place where the soil is black. It is the best soil in the country,' Tedros said; 'but ever since I was a child I used to think that yellow soil was better because it contained gold. Whenever I looked at Eritrea I always thought that because our soil was yellow then our country was very rich.'

'The soil in England is black. But I don't think it's that good. We use many chemicals on our soil. It causes a lot of pollution. The rivers go green in summer. They're disgusting.'

We sat there chatting, slowly picking out ideas or thoughts from our heads and trying them out on each other, a random conversation that continued as the wind whipped itself to a frustrated frenzy. The floating mountains of white cloud started moving towards us, turning from white to grey to black. Octopuses, slithering over the land on long tentacles of rain. When the storm broke, the rattle of fat raindrops on the roof was deafening, but still I could hear Tedros's quiet voice.

'Do you know Jeffrey Archer?' Tedros asked. 'I don't mean personally, but do you know of him?'

'Yes,' I said.

'I think he is very great,' Tedros said after a pause. 'One of the outstanding writers of the century. It is my opinion.'

'His books are popular, but I don't think he is well liked,' I told him.

'Yes, I heard he was in Parliament. I expected he would be prime minister. But then after his affair . . .' Tedros drifted off, and I followed his gaze out over Eritrea; then he started again, slowly. 'But when Mrs Thatcher said that he was one of the greatest writers this century, my friends and I all agreed.'

'Were they your friends in the Field?' I asked.

'No,' Tedros said, 'they were my friends when I was a prisoner.'

'I didn't know you were in prison.'

Tedros's line of sight stretched out past the horizon.

'I was in prison for fifteen years,' he said.

I went to see Tedros again the following week. His door was slightly ajar.

I knocked and peeped in.

Tedros was lying on the bed.

I saw his feet, hairy ankles, trousers and shirt, and his head shaded by a crooked arm. He was asleep, and the light of the door opening woke him. He jumped up, wide-eyed and startled. For an instant his face was twisted in fear and I stepped back.

'Sorry,' I said.

'No matter,' he said and turned away. When he turned back the look was gone, and all I saw was the bleary face of someone just woken up. He washed his face and pushed wet fingers through his hair.

'Sit down,' he said, and I did, but his eyes still disturbed me.

I'd been to Arregai's a few days before, and asked Arregai if he knew Tedros the fighter. He ordered two cappuccinos and pulled up a chair. We sat together; the machine gurgled as quietly as a drowning man and Arregai told me Tedros's story.

Tedros had been wounded in battle and captured by the Ethiopians. He was taken to the notorious prison in Asmara called Mariam Gumbe. It was where Awot's lover Selma had been tortured and killed seven months before liberation.

There, like her, Tedros was tortured. The interrogators beat him, deprived him of sleep, burnt him, confused him, dunked him into raw sewage, and beat him again – but even when he insisted that he'd told them everything they still asked for more.

The Ethiopians handed him over to an Eritrean torturer who worked for the secret police. The previous beatings had only been a warm-up for what Tedros now went through. And this time it was at the hands of a fellow-Eritrean, which hurt more. The intense pain, both physical and mental, made Tedros more determined. He would tell them nothing.

> *I have nothing to tell you*
> spitting blood from his mouth
> *I have nothing to tell you*
> as a cigarette ember burrowed into his skin
> half-drowned in filthy water
> gasping for breath
> vomiting
> *I have nothing to tell you*
> again, and again.

When the torturer had got everything he could out of Tedros he was marked down to be sent on to a proper prison in Addis Ababa. But before they let him go the Ethiopians had to break his defiance, if only for their own personal satisfaction. They would demonstrate that even though he hadn't told them everything, they still had power over his life. So, on the morning when he was going to be sent to Addis they tied him down and pulled down his trousers. His genitals were already covered with sores from electric shocks and burns, but as a parting present they went one step further. They used a kitchen knife to cut open his scrotum, pop each testicle out, one by one, and cut them off.

That day Tedros was sent to the Alembakka prison in Addis. It was where the Ethiopian regime stockpiled anyone who might threaten it. Tedros's story was remarkable because it was the standard story of people who were captured by the Ethiopians. Maybe he was 'lucky' because he had survived.

The name Alembakka meant 'Goodbye to the World'. People who went there stayed in for life. There were politicians, thinkers, writers, professors, doctors, generals and captured soldiers. They turned their life sentences into an opportunity to learn.

The prison became a university. There were professors and teachers as well as uneducated men. Within their walls they created faculties and courses. There were departments, and exams and degrees awarded. Everyone taught and studied at the same time. If you were studying for a maths degree, you taught high-school maths to others. While some graduated in biotechnology, wrote theses and dissertations, other prisoners began to learn to read and write. Education was a way of demolishing the walls that held them in.

———

Each year President Isaias Aferwerki celebrated Martyrs' Day in a different town of Eritrea. It was a day when all those who had died in the war were remembered.

Nineteen ninety-eight was Keren.

Workers erected a giant white candle, with an inverted tear-drop flame of yellow and red, on the slopes of Keren Fort. At night it was spotlit so that it shone. The sun set, silhouetting the ring of mountain peaks, then the cool midnight blue squeezed out the last drops of daylight and stars began to appear and a sliver of a moon hung over the black-blue peaks.

The main roundabout in the centre of Keren began to fill with people. More people kept coming from along the tributary roads. The white-robed women looked like silent ghosts, but close up their dark faces were alive with emotions: some smiling, others looking intent, and many sad.

People started passing round candles, till every hand held a candle, and every eye reflected back a thousand pinpoints of flame. Candles were even wedged into the crooks of branches or into bits of bark, the whole world just countless candle flames burning in the night as mothers and husbands, children and lovers, summoned back the dead to memory for a while.

It was an intensely personal moment for the Eritrean people. Not just fighters, not just the EPLF or ELF men, but for all the Eritreans. It was their struggle, their family members who had been killed, their sacrifices that had been made.

I left them behind and walked up to the post office and Arregai's in a trance. Police were clearing the road that President Isaias would come up when the ceremony was ended. It took me a while to comprehend what I was seeing. The policemen had long canes and were beating the people. One old man, frail and grey, strayed out of the crowd, not sure of what was going on. The police swept down on him; he crumpled under their blows as if each impact snapped his insides. A middle-aged man, maybe his son, came dashing out, arms raised, to try and steer his father to safety. The police saw him leave the crowd and fell upon the new target with renewed vigour. They left the old man, who was bleeding from his nose and scalp, and then thrashed his son to the floor.

I didn't want to see this, not on a night like tonight: it made me too angry; so I turned around and walked back to the circle of people. President Isaias was still talking about the sacrifices made during the struggle.

A woman I didn't know looked at me and smiled. I smiled back, and she took my arm softly, and gave me a candle. I don't know how long I stood there, ten minutes or two hours. All I remembered was the candle flames and the flames reflected in the silent eyes of dark faces. I had nothing to do with the struggle, but they wanted me there: as a witness.

After a while I decided it was time to leave them to their sadness, like closing the doors and letting a family grieve in private.

Seeing the old man and his son beaten up gave me a numb feeling that stayed with me for days, slowly fading from my bones until Tedros brought it back. He was strangely withdrawn.

'Thank you, Justin,' Tedros said as I gave him tea and sat with him under the tree by the staff office. 'Do you listen to *Outlook* on the BBC World Service?' he asked. 'They have a competition. I have the answers, right?'

'I'm not really sure,' I said, because I didn't know what the question was.

'I have a book, short story sunny time, am I right?' He was intent.

Deserted: Italian graveyard, Keren.

'I'm not sure,' I said confused.

It was the last time I saw Tedros. He was with his grand-mother when he did it. He poured kerosene over his head and set it alight. As he burnt he ran out into the street scream-ing, and people found him there. He had also stabbed himself in the stomach just to make sure.

It was both a very simple and grotesquely complex act. On

top of thirty years of death and loss and destruction; on top of the everyday grind of life; on top of the growing feeling of disappointment with liberation – this was another thing to bear.

I asked Tedros's friends why he had done it, but they were inured to death. They seemed to say merely, 'It's just another person dead, let's just carry on.' I was frustrated, but they had lost so many friends and loved ones that they couldn't grieve for them all.

I asked Habtewolde, and he took me for a long walk out into the burning plain, south of the town past the Italian tombs. The heat and the brightness dried up the pain a little, but the exhaustion of walking did more. After about three hours Habtewolde sat down under a lone acacia tree. He offered me a bottle of water which I gulped down.

He did not drink.

We sat in silence.

'Tedros's parents were trying to make him marry,' Habtewolde said suddenly. 'They wanted to keep up appearances, even though he could never have children. I think the pressure was too much.'

We walked home in silence and I though of Tedros as he went up in a smoke of kerosene and human flesh. We kept walking as the sun rolled down the sky and behind the mountains, and the night came rushing in.

Suicide – to choose death over life, not to exist over existing – can never make sense to the living.

That evening I sat on my veranda. The night shot insects at the lamp above my head, and they fell into my lap with singed wings. From the cluster of huts beyond the wall lamplight shone yellow, and the sound of a young boy reciting the

Koran stroked the air. I felt a mosquito on my knee and slapped it. There was blood on my hands; I wiped it clean and listened to the Arabic poetry of the Prophet Muhammad, Peace be upon Him.

————————

Ruth invited me round to her house again and I found my way there through the confused streets full of children and goats. She let me into her yard and we sat down for coffee under her tree, on a mat on the gravel painted with shadow. Terhas, a cousin, was there as well. Terhas was twenty-five or -six, and had been married for five years.

'Terhas has had a baby boy,' Ruth said.

Terhas was sitting on the mat with the boy lying on his back in front of her. She smiled at me, a warm white smile, and then she looked down at her baby. His body was rolled in fat, and his wide face cooed at the whisper of the leaves.

'How many now?' I asked Terhas.

'Four,' she smiled.

'Enough?'

'A few more,' she said.

Ruth roasted the coffee, and we smelt the strong dark smoke that was a caffeine rush in itself. As we sat, Terhas breastfed the baby. The baby's gums smacked and sucked on the nipple. A line of white dripped, to hang, a pearly drop of mother's milk, from his chin.

I had heard about so many atrocities from students and friends. Every day I saw the effects the war had on everyone still alive. I was beginning to see death and darkness everywhere. I had learnt so much about how cruel people could be to others, it was hard to think about it. Trying to understand the atrocities that had been carried out here, trying to understand the darker side of human nature, was like peering into a black hole. When I saw the baby feeding hungrily from Terhas's breast, a line of Homer sprang to mind. I say Homer, but it might have been Shakespeare; the image runs continually through history. You find it in Ancient Greece, the Bible, medieval or Victorian accounts, from the First and Second World Wars, and more recently in news reports from Bosnia: the image of plucking toothless babes from their mothers' nipples and dashing their brains out against a wall.

Ruth, Terhas, her baby and I sat and drank together. Ruth, always so positive, was quiet today. She said that life was hard at the moment. 'For all my years in the Field, the money is not enough. A student could have graduated while we were fighting and they can now earn more money than me. We fought for thirty years. We gave up our chance of education to fight the Ethiopians,' Ruth said straight. 'Many of us gave our lives.'

I nodded. She was right.

We both watched Terhas rock her babe backwards and forwards, then Ruth laughed. 'But we had the best kind of education!'

'Have you ever been back to Nakfa?' I asked her.

'No, not since liberation. I have not been back. You know, we spend all our money on surviving, we don't have money for anything else. We have to work all the time just to feed our families. Maybe in the future sometime.'

'Would you like to revisit the trenches?'

Ruth laughed at the idea. Some fighters had told me that they never wanted to go back to Nakfa, but others clearly missed it. Not necessarily the place, but all it stood for: the camaraderie, the struggle against impossible odds, the life when there was a tangible enemy to blame everything on, good and evil, black and white, the sense of being together.

'Would you *like* to go back to Nakfa?' I asked.

'Yes,' she said. 'My friends were only talking about it last week.' The trees rustled. Stormclouds threatened rain that never fell. 'Yes,' she told me. 'We miss Nakfa. We miss Nakfa a lot.'

VII

I spent Christmas in Keren. I bought a goat from the market in the riverbed, took him home and let him run free in my yard for a day. The next morning, after dawn, I dug a hole in the yard next to the tomato vines. He bleated loudly, scattering piles of black marbles wherever he shat.

I had my breakfast and a cup of tea. Then I went out for him.

I caught him by the horns and took him to the back of my house, tied his legs together, laid him flat on the ground. I went to the kitchen and took out my sharpest knife. It had been ground to a razor edge at the metalworking shop: sparks flying. The goat lay patiently on the ground. It didn't struggle. I knelt behind it, pulled its head back, exposed the long soft throat. It bleated once, brown eyes rolling back to look at me.

I picked up the knife.

The kid's muscles tensed as the blade peeled back skin and windpipe, arteries and then bone. There was a muffled gurgle; its eyes didn't move but they changed, looked wild. Its legs tried to kick but they couldn't. I put the knife between two vertebrae, and cut the spinal cord, then stood up as the blood pumped out into the dust.

When the blood had stopped I cut off the goat's head and

tossed it into the pit. Peeled-back lips left a grin of close white teeth. Like Achilles and Hector, I put thongs through its tendons and hung its dead body from the washing line. The stump of its neck dripped more blood on to the ground. The warm muscles came off the bone into a wide metal bowl.

Some friends came round and cooked him up in large pots, while I sat in the cool dark shade and tried to wash the smell of warm flesh from my hands.

I buried the skin with the head and tipped dust over them all. At lunchtime the guests arrived: Habtewolde, Dawit, Igzaw and other teachers from the school. They sat around each table and spread out the wide plates of injera. I tipped out ladles of zigne. The hot stew steamed while they washed their hands and prayed to God.

———

It was a bad summer that year.

It took a week for President Isaias Aferwerki to confirm the rumours. He appeared on TV, and the whole country stopped to watch him speak. Yes, he announced, after seven years of peace, there had been armed clashes between Eritrea and Ethiopia again. The unthinkable had happened: Ethiopian and Eritrean troops were again massing for war. Eritrean TV ran the President's announcement, and then a few Eritrean experts sat in armchairs and discussed the justification for the Eritrean claim.

'The Ethiopian forces came in and shot our officials in cold blood. We had to do something.'

'Yes,' they said; 'this land is Eritrean and will always be Eritrean.'

'We fought the Ethiopians before. We can fight them again.'

'We will stand up for what is right.'

'There are better ways to solve our problems, but if they want to fight then we are ready to fight.'

President Isaias came on, pulled a map out of his briefcase and pinned it to the studio wall.

'This is the disputed area on the map,' he said, pointing to a bit that had been coloured in with felt-tip. 'After the Ethiopian soldiers shot our officials in cold blood then we counter-attacked and killed a hundred Ethiopians.' He turned to the screen and said, 'We will not tolerate this Ethiopian aggression.

'We want peace,' he declared, and managed to rattle off a soundbite. 'I call on the Ethiopians to demilitarise the whole area and let international mediators solve the problem.'

But at the same time the Eritrean national servicemen and women were moved to their battle stations. Forty thousand youths had been conscripted into the National Development Campaign to dig irrigation across the country. They now turned in their picks and spades and took up guns again.

It was impossible to find out what the Ethiopians were saying, because the Eritrean newspapers ignored the stand-off completely, as if it wasn't happening. Everything was by word of mouth.

I went to see Awot. 'In fact it's not Ethiopia but Tigray Province which has invaded,' he told me. 'They are an autonomous region of Ethiopia.'

Tigray was the northern province of Ethiopia, once the lands of Ras Alula. The TPLF (Tigray People's Liberation Front) had worked together with the EPLF against Mengistu. They'd been allies for years, and after defeating Mengistu the

TPLF had become the Ethiopian government. The culture and language of the Tigray and Tigrinya were almost identical; only the Italian occupation separated them.

Indeed, President Isaias Aferwerki of Eritrea and President Meles Zenawi of Ethiopia were cousins.

Awot showed me an Italian map from the Fascist era. The map supported the Eritrean claims, and the Eritreans said that because the map had been made by the Italians, who were Europeans, then it was conclusive proof. The Ethiopians said the map was unreliable precisely because it had been made during the Fascist era, when the Italians had had territorial ambitions on Ethiopia.

The disputed land itself was an innocent and unassuming little wedge of highlands. Some people said it had a bit of gold, others that it was in the most fertile corner of Eritrea, the only bit of Eritrea that the satellite photograph showed as green. But neither gold nor grain supported the prospect of war.

Through the BBC World Service I learnt that the Ethiopians based their claim on a map they'd made with a German non-governmental organisation called GTZ, which had examined the written treaty rather than maps made from it. The GTZ map supported the Ethiopian claim, the land was Ethiopian not Eritrean.

The Ethiopians said that the Eritreans had been deliberately refusing to come to any decision about the border. They claimed the Eritreans had attacked. They said the Eritreans were occupying parts of Ethiopia. They said that if the Eritreans didn't leave Ethiopian territory then they would declare war.

In Keren Market the Bilen were criticising the Eritrean government.

'It was Eritrea who invaded Tigray first,' a friend at Arregai's told me, 'under one of our wartime generals.'

'Why?' I asked.

He told me his theory. It sounded as ridiculous as all the rest. Everyone had their own idea. There was a shopping list of why, when and how. I worked my way through most of them.

'It doesn't make sense,' I said.

'This is not logic, this is control,' the man told me. 'Why should we fight Ethiopia again? Because the government wants to use a crisis to clamp down opposition, to unify the people – how can we know?'

The restaurant owner wiped his hands on his white apron as he sat down and sipped sweet tea. He leant in so his other customers could not hear.

'Our leaders know nothing else but war,' he said. 'It's natural to them.'

The people discussed rumours as if they were messages from God. When I lay down at night and blew out the candle, I turned in the sheets and tried to forget all the things I'd heard. But each night, in the early hours, trucks and tanks on the Keren–Asmara road stampeded through town on their way to the battle stations and made the glass in my windows rattle.

The older people, people who had death branded into their psyches, were unanimous in declaring that they did not want war. They had had thirty years of it and that was enough. But the students and young people wanted to go and kill the 'bastard Ethiopians'. They said they would leave on a bus to the front tomorrow. They had learnt about the struggle for liberation at school. To die for Eritrea was their duty.

For the fighters, the war was almost a relief from the monotony of peace. The prospect set them off in secret conversations in the corners of rooms. The renewed sense of camaraderie, the proper order of life when there is a tangible enemy to fight, an enemy with a face you could kill, had bonded them together again. They said if they were ordered to fight they would fight.

I asked a mother why her son wanted to go and die for Eritrea.

'The young people see how well the fighters are treated, better than anyone else. They get all the good jobs, all the chances of going abroad to study. The young people see fighters are more respected than anyone else. So they want to go too. They have learnt that the only way to get honour is by fighting. In the seven years of peace that is the only thing the government has taught our children.'

Her husband shook his head. He was bald with a white beard and eyebrows, and black skin. He looked like a negative. He rubbed his scalp and cleared his throat before he spoke. He was used to being listened to.

'The young people have no jobs, no chance of getting a good job because they are not fighters. They have nothing else to do. No jobs, no education. When people have nothing to do then they fight. What we need for peace is jobs. We are not interested in countries or nationalism. Eritrea, Ethiopia – these are just names to us, they don't mean anything. We just want peace and food and money in our pockets. It is too simple for our government to understand.'

Awot looked fired up when we met for coffee. But when he spoke he sounded almost dazed by events. In three weeks

Eritrea had gone from being open allies with Ethiopia to being on the verge of war with them. I could only think of Orwell's *Nineteen Eighty-Four*: next the government would be telling us that we were allies with Sudan, that we had always been allied to Sudan, and that Ethiopia had always been our enemy.

'We are all sick of war,' Awot said. 'We have had war for thirty years, we know what war is.'

'Aren't the Ethiopians sick of it too?' I asked.

'No,' he said. 'I spent the morning listening to the Ethiopian radio. They're talking, talking, inciting their people to violence. I listened to a reporter go to an elementary school and talk to a young girl.

'"So what have you learnt in history?" he asked her.

'"We have learnt about the Battle of Adua, when the Italians and Eritreans tried to attack Ethiopia in the nineteen-hundreds," she said.

'"And what are you learning now?" he asked her.

'"Now we have learnt that the Eritreans want to attack again and take our country. I hope we beat the Eritreans."

'How can they teach their children this stuff? They will grow up with bad feelings towards their neighbours. Then the problem will last a hundred years.'

In Arregai's, the talk was that the war would be short but also very bloody. Everyone was sure it would happen. They were also sure they were right, and that they would win.

'We don't want war, but if they attack then we will go to fight,' said Berhane, slamming his fist on to the tabletop and spilling all the drinks. 'We will fight!'

I was sick of everyone talking like this was a football match. I saw all the hard work to rebuild Eritrea – the work of Awot or Nejat or even the work in our school, to rebuild a country and try to ensure that the people growing up there might have a better life – all this dedication and hard, hard work about to disappear.

I rationalised what was happening: in twenty years' time, or forty, or fifty, this war will be looked back on and seen as a constructive moment in the evolution of a country. Soon no one here will be alive. In a hundred years it'll be in a textbook, of no more importance than the Charge of the Light Brigade or the Battle of Gettysburg.

But each time I tried I came back to the fact that I was here. It was *my* life involved. I knew the victims intimately. I had friends who were at the front, friends who didn't have the protection of years.

Mobilisation was a daily event as new sectors of Eritrean society were called to the trenches. After ten days the government called up the EPLF fighters who had joined up in 1990, and had since been demobbed. They were delighted. They drove through Keren in the backs of lorries, cheering and waving to silent crowds. They were excited to be going back to war, even though their deaths waited for them there.

'They are brave fighters,' Berhane told me, 'because they are all well educated.'

'Aren't these educated people better off staying in their jobs?' I asked.

'But our government says that in Eritrea all people are equal,' he said. 'They must all fight.'

'But when there is peace, educated people will be needed to help in the reconstruction. Eritrea shouldn't waste its educated people,' I said, exasperated. 'There aren't many of them.

There are plenty of men here who are doing nothing. Why not save the educated people until last?'

Everyone around me seemed quite insane.

They made me feel that I was mad.

'This is our country,' Berhane said. 'We will fight for it.'

If anyone was against the war I thought it would be Adam. I remembered how he'd said that he never even wanted to see a gun again.

I found him sitting in the street, trying to rub the bright sunlight from his head.

'I'll never drink at lunchtime again,' he said.

I asked him if he would go back to war or not.

'Of course!' He brightened up. 'When I am ordered to, I will go to fight the bastard Ethiopians.'

'You said that you never wanted to see a gun again,' I told him.

'Yes, but this is my country,' he said.

I didn't feel let down by his answer, just more and more excluded, a spectator to a process that didn't concern me. With each answer I felt that I had less in common with these people, as if they were a different species from me. I asked Adam why there was fighting. After thirty years weren't the people sick of war?

'Yes,' he said. 'But if the Ethiopians want to fight then we will fight!'

'People always say that,' I answered. 'But they always sound as if *they* want to fight.'

He stood up. 'We do not want to fight. I do not want to fight. I do not want to kill. In seven years we have worked so hard to develop. It is easy to destroy, very easy! Even to kill, you can kill a man like this –' he clicked his fingers – 'it is so easy. But to rebuild takes such a long time. What we need now is to build, not to destroy. I do not want war.'

———

The summer rains broke the same day that the war started. Black clouds from the Gulf of Guinea rolled over the land, a vast cloud of boiling smoke blotting out the mountains. The first fat drops rattled on the tin roofs, gunshot-loud, then the deluge came as a deafening roar.

I had hardly slept because of the rumble of heavy traffic driving through town all night long. Eritrean roads had never been designed to take troop trucks or tanks, and through the night I had listened to the rattle of the door and windows on their hinges. When daylight squeezed through the chinks in the shutters I got up from my fitful sleep and turned on the radio.

It was the World Service, from London.

'Eritrea and Ethiopia have gone to war,' a voice said. 'Both sides have reported thousands of casualties.'

While the radios of the world were announcing in a hundred different languages that the three-week stand-off had ended, Eritrean Radio was still talking about the achievements of the National Development Campaign. So many hectares of land brought under the plough. So many miles of irrigation channels dug. How the desert would bloom.

I walked to the Ministry of Education office through the rain.

'I've heard that the war's started,' I shouted to Faffa over the din of the rain on the tin roof. He was listening to a radio on the desk in front of him. The antenna was a length of wire pinned to the map of Eritrea. He unplugged the Walkman earphones from his ears.

'Eh?' he said.

'War,' I said.

He nodded and wiped his sweaty fingers on his dirty T-shirt. 'I know. The government wants me to close the elementary schools and send the teachers to the front.'

'How about the exams?'

'They haven't told me what to do about exams. I'm sure they'll think of something,' he said, and let out a long sigh. 'What will you do now?' he asked.

'I'm not sure,' I said. 'I thought I'd go for a coffee.'

Faffa frowned at me. 'You'll have to wait for the rain to stop,' he said, sitting back.

I did, outside his door, on the veranda. Over the dusty road there was another villa that was crumbling back into the ground. It had once been the most beautiful villa in Keren. Now its terracotta-tiled roof was patched with tin, the statue of Cupid in the fountain had been shattered by gunfire and a tank had demolished part of the garden wall. On the soft ochre brickwork of the villa wall was an incongruously new grey marble sign that said MAJOR GENERAL GEBRESELASSIE HAILE-MARIAM – an Ethiopian officer's declaration from the time of Mengistu that he was here to stay.

I looked across the dirt road and saw the children running wild with the goats. As the fat droplets walloped them on the head they squealed with delight and ran for cover. One little boy, terrified by the rattle of raindrops, stood stock still and cried as the rain splashed dirt up his legs. His mother came dashing out from under the veranda and gathered him up to safety.

The rain fell and I stood and watched the long streams of water stretch the windowpanes. The storm reached a crescendo of white sound and the drums of thunder battered in the sky. In less than five minutes water overflowed the broken gutters and the road was awash.

'Are you going to celebrate?' Habtewolde asked with a bright smile, as he held out his hand.

I turned towards him. 'No, certainly not.'

'Why not?'

'It's terrible.'

'Why? It happens to everyone.'

'Not very often.'

'It happens every year,' he smiled.

'Not in England.'

'Don't be shy,' he chided.

I was confused.

'It's your birthday,' he said, slapping my arm.

Oh yes.

'I thought you were talking about the war,' I said.

His face went very serious. He nodded. 'Yes, those terrible Ethiopians again,' he said. 'I have prayed for victory.'

The days when we heard nothing dragged on interminably. Four days felt like a month. We swapped rumours about the war: where the clashes were, who was winning.

A distant bang! bang! bang! disturbed my sleep. There was someone outside calling my name. I was sure I didn't recognise the man's voice. I got up and opened my gate, and found the strange man had climbed back into his car to look at his map.

'Justin Hill?' he shouted as he jumped back down.

'Yes?' I said.

'I'm from the embassy. You have twenty minutes to pack,' he told me. 'I'm evacuating you.'

Children came and watched me load up the embassy's four-wheel-drive. The man kept hurrying me along. There was no time for goodbyes. As I was driven out of town I saw Habtewolde in the street and leant out of the car and waved.

'Stop!' I told the driver. 'Stop!

'They're evacuating me,' I told Habtewolde as I jumped out on to the road. 'They're evacuating me.'

We shook hands and hugged. He wasn't emotional, but I was. I felt I was abandoning him – and my friends and students and even the people around me I didn't know. 'I'm sure I'll be back,' I said. 'I'll probably just be in Asmara for a week or so.'

Habtewolde nodded. The driver was beeping his horn. We hugged again and I left him there in the street.

We drove through the dark along the winding mountain road to Asmara. The world was only as big as the area illuminated by the headlights. Wrecks of tanks from the last war lined the road, and it felt like we were driving back through the debris of a nightmare, and into another.

'We are all sick of war. We have had war for thirty years, we know what war is,' the driver told me.

'Aren't the Ethiopians sick of it too?' I asked for what felt like the hundredth time.

The main streets of Asmara were quiet. The government radio said nothing about the conflict, but Eritrea was too small to keep secrets in. Everyone knew what was happening, and they braced themselves for it. War fit them like an old uniform. They walked with shoulders straight, bearing the trials that were to come. They were sure that they were right, and that they would beat the Ethiopians.

Most people probably think that when they go to war.

Unlike the Eritreans, most foreigners in town were frenetic, rushing about trying to find out what the hell was happening. The British Embassy for Eritrea was in Addis Ababa, and so an environmental consultant was made Consul for the week to get us all out. He was a tall young man with round shoulders and a nonchalant air. He had a leather bag slung over his shoulder that he never opened.

'What's happening?' we asked.

He shrugged.

'When will we be evacuated?'

'I don't know.'

He didn't seem to know much at all.

The only place where news was free and easy to come by was the American Embassy. They posted bulletins whenever the situation changed. The words held ominous warnings of what might happen.

JUNE 4TH

VOLUNTARY EVACUATION ORDER FOR ALL
AMERICAN CITIZENS AND DEPENDANTS.
WEIGHT ALLOWANCE 85 LBS.

The next morning I went for a coffee and bumped into an Irish guy called Billy who used to work in Elaboret. He was sitting with a blue ice-cream and a caffè latte; he looked depressed.

'What do you know?' I asked as I sat down.

He looked at me. 'I know,' he said firmly, 'that I'm not going to enjoy 1998.'

He sat watching his ice-cream melt. 'They're Fascists,' he said at last. 'Fucking Fascists. What the fuck do they think they're doing?' I watched an Eritrean woman walk past with a bag of vegetables. 'I don't understand how they can do it. They are too *awful* for words.'

Billy really did look depressed, so after breakfast we went for a walk through the streets of Asmara to enjoy the Art Deco capital of the world.

We came across an old poster for the National Development Campaign. It showed a foot transmuting into a hand that was holding up a spade. There was no ankle.

'Now look at this,' Billy said, pointing at the poster. 'This is not art, it's ugly.'

'I wonder what's the message of this poster,' I asked. 'It looks more like a warning of the dangers of radioactivity.'

Billy looked at me, and then gave a glance over his shoulder at the Eritreans looking at us looking at the poster.

'The message of this poster,' he said, 'is *not* to look at this poster.'

JUNE 5TH
MEETING FOR ALL US CITIZENS AT 9 A.M.
SITUATION HAS DETERIORATED FURTHER.
INVOLUNTARY EVACUATION ORDER.
CHARTER FLIGHT 11 P.M. THIS EVENING.
ASSEMBLE AT AIRPORT BY 10 P.M.
BAGGAGE ALLOWANCE 2 SUITCASES, MAX. 40 LBS.

At two-thirty in the afternoon on 5 June everything was quiet. People were sleeping off lunch while I sat in the Consulate garden, talking with friends. There was a low screech over town, a dull thud then a sound of *ak-ak-ak*. Another blast.

Then silence. You had to pinch yourself to be sure it had happened. We looked at each other in disbelief and confusion.

The Ethiopians had started bombing Asmara.

There was no warning, no crescendo of the orchestra. Just normal life, bombs dropping and somewhere people shredded by explosions of flying metal, then quiet and normality again.

The phone rang almost immediately. Everyone was to assemble and wait. We were going to be airlifted out.

EVACUATION!

FLIGHT BROUGHT FORWARD TO 7 P.M.

ASSEMBLE AT US EMBASSY.

ONE PIECE HAND LUGGAGE ONLY.

British and Canadian citizens assembled at the British Consulate. The front garden was full of bags and confused people, plucked from their communities at a moment's warning.

'One piece of hand luggage only,' we were ordered.

I looked at my luggage: books and tapes, short-wave radio, clothes, photos, shoes, washbag. I tried to decide how much I could get into my piece of hand luggage, and gave up. It was pointless. I packed some soap, a book, my toothbrush, toothpaste and deodorant. At least I would have clean teeth and something to read.

Some people were hysterical. Others were rushing off to get their last Melottis. Others just sat quietly, hugging each other and crying.

Through the long afternoon we waited for the telephone call to say that the first evacuation plane had landed. I still clung on to the dream of rebuilding Eritrea. The governments would opt for a peaceful settlement because it was the only thing that made sense.

It was a long, tense wait. Suddenly we could hear a car coming closer, giving a news announcement. I listened but couldn't make out what had happened. It was certainly causing a celebration. Cars were hooting their horns and people were blowing whistles.

I ran out on to the street. People were dancing and waving flags, cars were hooting their horns.

'Why's everyone dancing?' I asked a passer-by. But he was too excited and ran past me into the crowd.

'Why is everyone dancing?' I was almost laughing as I asked a woman, who was singing and clapping her hands. She didn't answer as she danced past. I was almost dancing myself.

'What's happened?' I asked a schoolgirl with dreadlocks and a bag of homework over her shoulder.

'We have shot down one of the Ethiopian jets!' she told me, before rushing off to join the crowds. 'We have captured a pilot!'

The young people of Asmara beat drums, whistled and waved flags. Passing cars hooted their horns. They had something to celebrate.

We got our telephone call at six-fifty. Ten minutes later we were all on a bus to the airport with our single pieces of

Ethiopian jet shot down.

hand luggage. The bus was silent except for a few sobs. We all stared out of the windows and tried to fix Eritrea in our heads.

We arrived at the airport at 7.30 p.m.

A group of young, confused officials from the US State Department met our bus. The Assistant Ambassador stood a little way off and smiled in a bemused way. His calm was totally opposite to his staff. Their nerves were already shot through, and they bounced off each other like panicked molecules in Brownian motion.

A woman called Mary climbed on to the bus. 'OK, guys – don't jerk me round,' she started. 'Just fill in the blue forms, and you're going to do it NOW!'

'What blue forms?' someone shouted.

'You don't have blue forms?' she gasped. 'Oh my God, Tom,' she said as she climbed off the bus. 'I can't deal with this.'

There was a moment of silence, then she climbed back up. 'OK, listen, you guys, you need to get the BLUE FORMS,' she said. 'We'll give them to you when you get off the bus. I'll call out your names one by one, and get off the bus as quickly as you can!'

She started reading out the names. It was a painfully slow business. We began to realise how exposed we were, parked on a runway that was about to be bombed. Someone else took over. It was another woman, with a blonde ponytail.

'OK, guys, just do as you're told,' she said. 'GET OFF the bus, and then we'll give you your BLUE FORMS!'

We helped each other off and distributed the BLUE FORMS.

Mary was leaning against the bus, rubbing her head and swearing. 'Oh my God, oh my God.' Then she looked up and started shouting at us again. 'Come on, guys, this is a WAR situation. We need you to be very, very quick! I need your BLUE FORMS. When you have completed the blue forms then proceed to the FRONT.'

We filled in the blue exit forms. Mary hopped and screamed and called out names and contradictory commands one after the other.

'Come to the FRONT!' she shouted.

'Leave the BLUE forms!' another said.

'DO the blue forms!'

'Go THROUGH the gates!'

We forgot about the Ethiopian jets and the war, and our

friends, and someone started laughing so hard they had to sit down.

We gave in our blue forms and were herded together. Our passports were taken from us, then we were rushed across the tarmac to the plane. Inside, nobody was crying or shouting. We sat in silence.

It was 8 p.m. when we took off. The sun had set, and the lights of the city were on.

I stared down at Asmara as we gained height and left it behind, burning in the darkness till the light faded away to darkness.

Eritrea was returning to war and we were leaving them to it.

———

The plane travelled north along the Nile. I didn't sleep all night. Beneath us in the blackness I watched the towns and villages of Egypt come into view, strung out along the banks, watched as we followed them north.

From thirty-five thousand feet the lines of lights made a filigree necklace of diamonds.

We were returning to the real world.

There was a group of twelve US military advisers sitting at the back of the plane with crew-cuts and muscles bursting out of their clothing. They were complaining because, as it was a Muslim-owned plane, there was no alcohol on board.

'I need a fucking beer,' one said.

'Too fucking right, man!'

'Let's take over the plane and force them back to Asmara. We can load up on beers!'

They all laughed: deep pectoral laughter.

When we landed at Cairo everyone got up and chatted like someone had just released us all from solitary confinement. The stewardesses opened the cabin doors as we refuelled; the warm breeze of Cairo smelt so different to that of Eritrea.

The plane took off again, and the Egyptian pilot made a joke about a safer take-off than we'd just had. Everyone laughed. I laughed so much I started crying.

We flew through the night to Frankfurt Airport, and got off into a dull European dawn in cotton clothes bleached pale by the Eritrean sunlight. We passed through empty lounges in the haunted hours of early morning. Waiting for a connection to London, we watched the cleaning staff arriving out of the lifts. At five-thirty the McDonald's opened.

When we arrived at Heathrow it was still so early in the morning that only television film crews were there to welcome us. I phoned a friend, but she was out. I wanted to talk to someone just to prove to myself that I was still alive and awake and back in England.

I phoned my mother. She asked me how I was. I said OK.

'It must have been terrible,' she said. 'Why are they fighting?'

'I don't know.'

'Why are they always fighting over there?' she asked. 'Well, it'll be nice to have you back,' she said, 'and at least you're all right – that's what's important.'

We all stood together for a while, then people began to organise getting home or to friends' houses. Mothers or brothers or fathers arrived: running, crying, hugging, kissing. They shook hands and kissed again, said, 'How are you? It's so good to have you back.'

I bought a ticket to Leeds–Bradford Airport. As I waited I started thinking what I could do now that I was back in the UK.

I sat and there was an announcement that the flight to Leeds–Bradford had been cancelled due to bad weather. I went up to the British Midland desk, where a crowd of people were complaining about the cancelled flight. Others were moaning about the weather, which was, so they said, the worst summer they could remember.

I asked for an alternative flight to the nearest airport to York.

'Newcastle?' the lady said politely.

'Fine,' I said.

'Check-in time is on the card. Non-smoking,' she told me.

'Thanks.'

I flew up to Newcastle. The British Midland plane came down out of the clouds, and through the drizzle-streaked window I could see a dreary English landscape. It felt alien and powerfully reassuring at the same time. The rain-soaked fields were impossibly green; the cows that dotted the patchwork looked obese. I remembered the herds of shrink-wrapped toastracks that boys had driven out into the Keren hills. It was hard to think they were the same animals.

The plane landed and we walked into the terminal to collect our luggage. I saw my reflection in a glass door and was shocked: brown skin, bleached blond hair and faded trousers.

The first thing I would have to do would be to buy some new clothes.

I stood waiting and watching the test match against South Africa on an overhead TV screen. I looked at the other people waiting for their luggage and wondered if they could see anything strange about me, apart from my tan and my shabby, sun-bleached clothes. I worried that they could tell I'd just come from Eritrea and that they would ask me about the war or the evacuation. I didn't want to talk about it.

As I stood there I felt the billions of 'foreigners' outside Britain return to their appropriate distance. Not flesh and blood, only numbers in the newspapers, faces on the TV. Not real people, just figures starving, protesting, dying, rioting, dead.

Then I heard the roar of a passenger jet taking off outside, and I had a panic attack: the thud-thud-thud of bombs dropping, anti-aircraft fire, the white puff of a distant explosion under a hot blue sky.

There was a flash of news at 10 a.m. which had a brief report about the war. I stood and watched myself on the TV report walk out of the plane and across the screen, confused and smiling and glad to be back. The report said that there were still British nationals in Asmara, and that the war was escalating. A US and Rwandan peace plan had been accepted on principle by both sides, but they were still sending more troops to the front.

I bought a newspaper which had a picture from yesterday's fighting of two dead Ethiopian soldiers, mouths wide open, stretched on their backs and lips peeled back over dead white grins.

———

I was silent during the drive back to York. I missed my dog when I opened the door: he'd been put down a few months earlier. My mum put on the kettle and I carried my bags upstairs, dropped them in my old bedroom, went back down to the kitchen and stood, feeling that I should be somewhere else.

'Sit down,' my mum said. 'I'll make you a cup of tea.'

I sat.

'It's nice to have you back,' she said.

'It's nice to be back,' I said.

She came and put her arms around me and we hugged. She gave me an extra squeeze. 'What would you like me to cook?' she asked.

'Oh, I don't mind,' I said.

'How about bacon sandwiches?' she said.

'OK,' I said. 'Listen, I think I'll just go upstairs for a lie-down.'

'All right.'

The news I read in the papers was written by correspondents who had just flown in to cover the story. They knew less than anyone who'd been there, said nothing they couldn't have learnt from London. I wrote an article about the war and why it was happening, phoned up a few editors. A woman at *The Times* said she was interested.

'I'm fascinated about the idea of two old allies suddenly going to war,' she said. 'Can you do something on that angle?'

I angled it and faxed it the next day. She phoned me back.

'I've got your fax,' she said. 'I want to say I think it's really good. But I'm afraid we can't publish. I wanted to tell you in case you want to try other papers. But really I think they'll say the same because Eritrea and Ethiopia aren't in the news any more. The big story at the moment is about the football.'

'What football?' I asked.

'The World Cup,' she said. 'Some English football fans have started rioting in Marseilles. No one's interested in Eritrea any more. I can't run the piece. Sorry.'

VIII

The Asmara Restaurant is the converted front room of a terraced house in Brixton. There is red wallpaper on the walls, and curtains of raw cotton embroidered in gold and blue with the design of the Coptic cross. A picture of Asmara Cathedral hangs on the wall.

The owner of the restaurant is a small, gold-toothed woman called Abrahet. She tells me that most of the clients are English, not Eritrean. 'The Eritreans don't come here; they can get their food at home,' she says, nodding her head and smiling.

This evening the only two other customers are both Eritrean men. They sit alone facing the window and watching people pass by on the pavement outside. When Abrahet goes back into the kitchen I drink my coffee, strong and sweet, Eritrean-style, and watch them.

They do not talk, or even move. They look out of the window, watching the people pass in the grey London street. Thinking.

For two years I have followed the news from Eritrea. It is the kind of war that only gets coverage when there's nothing else to talk about: the dark note of the silly season. There have been sporadic reports from the front line, where modern weaponry, combined with First World War tactics and Victorian medical facilities, have made gruesome reading. A modern-day Passchendaele, it has been a continuous process of feeding ill-trained conscripts into the path of bullets, shells and landmines.

Today I read on the internet that after two years of fighting Ethiopian forces have finally broken through the Eritrean lines, and are overrunning the Eritrean lowlands. Both governments have finally agreed to a ceasefire. United Nations peacekeepers are to be deployed along the border. A UN committee will be appointed to decide on the issue of the border.

I sit and watch rush-hour people hurry across the front of the restaurant, pour another cup of coffee, add a spoonful of sugar, Eritrean style.

In the last two years I have written letters to my friends in Eritrea, but all of them have gone unanswered. I don't write any more.

There is some small satisfaction that Eritrea has been defeated in this war – the country may glory less in its military past – but most of all there is satisfaction and relief that the war will end. I sit and think of my friends and what will have happened to them. I imagine how they have reacted to the news that their soldiers are routing, and how many of their stories will have ended somewhere in the trenches and hospitals along the Eritrea–Ethiopia border. Most of all I am angry that the future we hoped and worked for turned so sour, but my involvement with Eritrea is such a short and insignificant part of the country's history. The Eritreans have suffered fear for a generation: but even after thirty years of war their spirit is not just unbroken, but positive and determined. There are many Awots or Ruths or Habtewoldes in Eritrea – many people like them across the world, in Africa, Asia, Europe and the Americas. People who suffer needless terror and persecution and use their strength to establish a better way of living. It is a small and often unnoticed contribution: but there can hardly be a better way to use our lives.

This is just a book, but the people and their stories are real. I hope their stories are a testament to the dreams we all had, which sparkled for a short while in the hot sun of Eritrea.